How to Boost Your IQ

How To Boost Your IQ

John Bremner

WARD LOCK

The opinions expressed in this book are those of John Bremner,
not of Mensa Ltd., as Mensa has no opinions.

Acknowledgements

I would like to thank my family and friends and all the volunteers who
racked their brains trying out the tests in this book, for their help and
encouragement. In particular, thanks to Robert and Martin Buckley for
their computer knowledge, and to Ian Sinclair for helping to uncover
mistakes and inconsistencies. Thanks also to Lydia Derbyshire for her
meticulous editing.

A Ward Lock Book
First published in the UK 1996
by Ward Lock
Wellington House
125 Strand
LONDON
WC2R 0BB

A Cassell Imprint

Copyright © John Bremner 1995

Reprinted 1996

The right of John Bremner to be identified as the author of this book has been
asserted by him in accordance with the provisions of the UK Copyright, Designs
and Patents Act 1988.

Distributed in the United States
by Sterling Publishing Co., Inc.
387 Park Avenue South, New York, NY 10016–8810

A British Library Cataloguing in Publication Data block for this book may be
obtained from the British Library.

ISBN 0 7063 7305 7

Typeset by Ben Cracknell Studios
Printed and bound in Great Britain by Cox & Wyman Ltd, Reading, Berkshire.

Contents

••••••••••••••••••••••••••••••••••

Introduction 6
IQ Test 1 9
Preparing for Tests 22
    Speed Reading 28

Verbal and Linguistic Ability 33
    Practice Test 35

Numerical Ability 49
    Numerical Practice Test 1 52
    Numerical Practice Test 2 57
    Numerical Practice Test 3 61

Visual–Spatial Ability 66
    Visual-Spatial Practice Test 1 74
    Visual-Spatial Practice Test 2 84

Principles of Logic 92
    Logical Deduction Practice Test 1 99
    Logical Deduction Practice Test 2 102
    Logical Deduction Practice Test 3 107

General Knowledge 111

IQ Test 2 123

Answers 136
Useful Addresses 144

Introduction

● ●

Imagine all the stars in the milky way; then imagine that each of them has 10,000 connections to other stars. If you have a good imagination, you have just constructed a limited mental model of your brain's neural network – limited, because within your brain there are more neurons than there are stars in this galaxy. Every time we form a thought, we make or strengthen chemical, physical and electrical connections between these neurons. The more connections there are, the faster and better our brain's communication system operates.

There are few limitations on the potential of each individual, which is something I can vouch for from personal experience. I failed my 11+ exam, and my parents were told that I would never achieve anything. But I am stubborn and decided early on not to be limited by other people's perceptions of me. I set about improving my mind and aimed for what, then, was the seemingly impossible target of achieving membership of Mensa, the high IQ society. Candidates must finish in the top two per cent in a recognized and supervised IQ test. Mensa give two tests: one with a pass mark of 133 and the other of 148.

To achieve that goal, I continually strove for mental improvement, until, some time ago, I achieved membership of Mensa. For some people, who perhaps will struggle less to achieve the same, that may mean little, but it gave me an immense feeling of satisfaction. However, since I am addicted to learning, the improvement process is continuing, and every day I realize that I can do something faster or better, and I achieve new insights into problems that previously baffled me.

Additional benefits are a heightened awareness of everything that goes on in the world and a new understanding and happiness, while my study and development of memory improvement techniques has reawakened much that I thought was lost to me. As my ability to think forwards has improved, so has my ability to think backwards, and this has occurred to an almost unbelievable extent.

We are all different, with different aptitudes and different potentials for improvement, so I cannot promise that this book will do the same for you. I can promise, however, that if you follow the instructions and take the necessary actions you will:

- increase your measurable IQ score
- increase your personal effectiveness
- release hidden creative powers
- get to know yourself a lot better
- develop greater versatility of mind
- gain new insights into the world at large
- improve your reasoning powers
- increase your attention span
- improve your memory and powers of concentration
- think faster and more accurately.

Some psychologists claim that there is a limit beyond which our intelligence cannot be developed, but even if that is true there are still many things under our own control that do not depend upon pure intelligence. It is, for example, much harder to measure qualities such as creative ability; potential for personal happiness; individuality and social intelligence; strength of mind and determination; work- and hobby-related skills; and personal understanding and compassion. These can be developed without limit, and in many ways they are far more important than 'pure' intelligence – if there is such a thing.

If you develop your creative ability, you will have a more flexible mind and skills that carry over into everyday life. Painting and drawing help to develop visual/spatial ability. Music has been found to stimulate the same brain areas that are used to solve problems. If you have strength of mind and determination, you will be able to apply those qualities to your studies and you will learn more. If you have work- and hobby-related skills, whether they are in mechanics, computing, writing, law or whatever, you will find that those skills contribute in some way to your measurable IQ. Nothing we learn is ever wasted. Nothing is fixed. Everything is possible. I believe that with all my heart, and I hope that by the time you finish this book, you will believe it too.

John Bremner

Test Instructions

- To provide the best possible estimate of your IQ, do not look at the test pages until you are ready to begin. Pre-viewing will falsely increase your score.

- Choose a quiet, well-lit place where you will not be disturbed.

- Have a few sheets of paper and two pencils ready.

- Do not write on this book if you intend to retake the test later. Instead, jot the question numbers and your solutions on a separate sheet. (Allow an extra 5 minutes for this.)

- Time will be short. The test has been designed so that few people will complete it in the time allowed. Don't waste time trying to do problems that you find difficult, but pass quickly to the next problem and come back to them later if you've time.

- Read the questions carefully.

- The answers section contains explanatory tips that should help you to see where, if anywhere, you went wrong.

- Use reading glasses if you need them. Observation is tested.

- Time allowed: 45 minutes. The time should be strictly adhered to.

- Remember that if you cheat, you are only cheating yourself.

IQ Test 1

45 MINUTES

● ●

Read the instructions on page 8 before beginning.

1. Underline the word inside the brackets that is closest to the meaning of the word outside the brackets. Example: give (push, hold, send, <u>donate</u>, gift).

   a. stir (mix, dizzy, whirl, round, soup)
   b. discuss (refer, consider, shout, agree, conference)
   c. further (away, gone, more, distance, remote)
   d. toss (throw, spin, shake, shoot, project)
   e. top (above, over, uppermost, high, height)

2. Solve the following.

   a. What day would today be if three days before Monday was the day before yesterday?
   b. What day would today be if four days ago tomorrow would have been Monday?
   c. What day would today be if three days ago yesterday would have been Tuesday?
   d. What day would tomorrow be if six days from now yesterday would be Wednesday?

3. Insert the missing numbers.

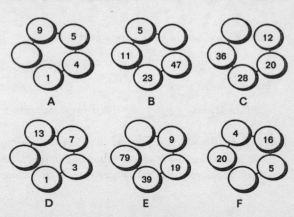

4. Which is the odd one out – A, B, C or D – from each of the following sets of objects?

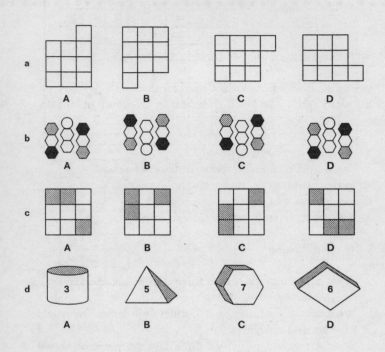

5. Complete the following sentence, selecting words from the list supplied. (Some of the words in the list will not be needed.)

Electricity is one of the cleanest and most _____ sources of

_____ in our world, but it can be very _____ to the

unwary. It has a way of _____ out the careless or the

indifferent and _____ them for their attitude.

cheapest, punishing, persistent, useful, heating, hitting, alive, looking, electric, annoying, dangerous, frightening, energy, cooking, electrocuting, seeking, distracting, angry, intense, lecturing.

6. Which tile comes next?

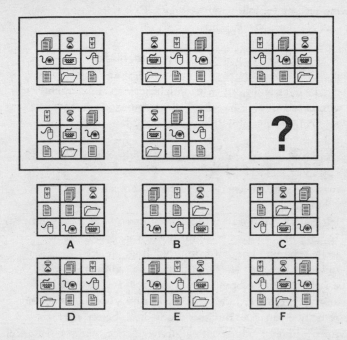

7. If $mb \times mc = b$ and $a + t = s + t$, which of the following statements are true (T) and which are false (F)?

a. $a + s = t + t$

b. $mb = b \div mc$

c. $mb \times b = mc$

d. $mc \times mb - b = 0$

e. $(a + t) - (s + t) = 0$

f. $a = s$

g. $a + t - s = t$

h. $mc \times b = mc$

i. $(a + t) \div (s + t) = (a \div s) + t$

j. $mb \times mc + (a + t) = (s + t) + b$

k. $mb \times mc + (a + t) = (s + t) \times b$

8. Underline the most suitable word from those within the brackets to complete each of the following analogies. Example: scissors ~ cut : dagger ~ (kill, slice, attack, <u>stab</u>).

a. snow ~ white : coal ~ (fire, burn, hard, black)

b. pencil ~ write : finger ~ (thumb, nail, point, soft)

c. dark ~ light : morning ~ (midnight, day, evening, night)

d. winter ~ summer : heaven ~ (sky, ground, earth, hell)

e. rejoicing ~ triumph : despondence ~ (glum, moody, morose, failure)

f. confusion ~ doubt : understanding ~ (know, certainty, consider, decide)

g. master ~ slave : owner ~ (property, dominate, cruel, submissive)

h. left ~ right : northeast ~ (northwest, southwest, east, southeast)

i. bad ~ good : morose ~ (optimistic, clear, healthy, dark)

j. jostle ~ bump : grab ~ (drop, hold, hug, pluck)

k. outcry ~ screech : secret ~ (keep, hush, whisper, reveal)

l. excel ~ forfeit : eclipse ~ (win, displace, fail, dissipate)

m. abstract ~ remove : annul ~ (break, ruin, abolish, obliterate)

n. remedy ~ panacea : throat ~ (body, heal, better, neck)

o. infer ~ imply : judgement ~ (jury, evidence, witness, sentence)

9. Find the missing numbers.

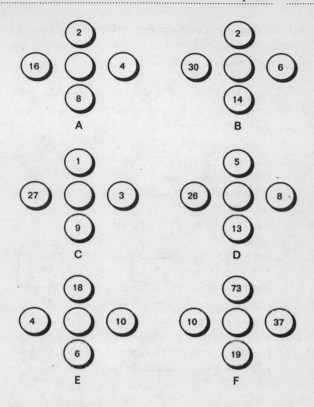

10. Find the prefixes that, when placed before each of the following groups of letters, will create valid words. Each set of words has a different prefix. Example: −ad, −eple, −reo, become stead, steeple, stereo with the prefix ste−.

a. −at,   −bal,   om,   −rify,   −rious,   −ssy
b. −nign,   −siege, −st,   −little, −stow,   −nt
c. −re,   −rge,   −nch,   −nish,   −rity,   −ny
d. −ill,   −im,   −inny,   −irt,   −ulk,   −y
e. −ll,   −pe,   −wry,   −t,   −ck,   −or
f. −of,   −t,   −tlit,   −ut,   −il,   −ok
g. −ng,   −nk,   −ght,   −sk,   −ttle,   −be
h. −st,   −ult,   −t,   −ry,   −unt,   −ried
i. −unt,   −ob,   −ue,   −ur,   −ink,   −ood
j. −ct,   −il,   −n,   −int,   −st,   −le

11. Which is the odd one out in each of the following sets?

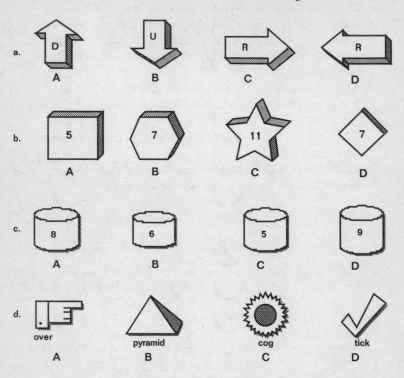

12. There are 21 birds in an aviary. One-seventh of the bird population are green. There are twice as many brown birds as green birds, and there are half as many brown birds as blue birds. A total of 12 birds can fly, but only one-third of those that can fly are under one year old, and only one-quarter of those that can fly are over two years old.

Which of the following statements are certainly true? (T)

Which of the following statements are possible but not necessarily true? (P)

Which of the following statements are certainly false? (F)

a. There are four times as many blue birds as green birds.

b. Two-thirds of those that can fly are between one and two years old.

c. The blue birds eat more food than the green birds.

d. Four of the birds under one year old can fly.
e. There are four birds over two years old that can fly.
f. There are three times more blue birds than there are green birds.
g. The blue birds are more successful at breeding than the green birds.
h. The green birds are the least successful birds.
i. Fewer than half of those that can fly are between one and two years old.
j. The owner of the birds prefers blue birds to green or brown birds.
k The aviary is large enough to accommodate 21 birds.
l. Between them, the birds have 42 feet and 126 toes.

13. Find the missing words selecting from the list below. Example: see, <u>sight</u>, view.

a. past, ____, future
b. hurt, ____, sore,
c. speak, ____, say
d. grip, ____, grasp
e. firm, ____, durable
f. sweet, ____, sour
g. high, ____, low
h. kick, ____, sole
i. beat, ____, slap
j. anger, ____, fear
k. miss, ____, hit
l. need, ____, want
m. push, ____, move
n. rare, ____, weird
o. birth, ____, death

Choose from: hold, desperation, strike, require, chatter, direct, lies, foot, mountain, time, talk, mendacity, altitude, declare, emotion, gritty, thump, strange, shape, taste, unforgettable, toe, condiment, pain, week, test, hit, seize, mad, chop, fight, life, aim, shift, tough

14. A man with only 500 black and 500 white hairs on his head, makes the fortunate discovery that for each white hair he pulls out, two black hairs and one white hair instantly grow back. He has thus found a method of replacing his hair.

a. How many hairs does he have to pluck to have 1,500 black hairs?
b. If he plucks 1,000 white hairs, how many hairs in total will he have?

c. How many times does he have to pluck out all his white hair to have 4,000 hairs in total.

d. If he initially pulls out only 200 white hairs, how many black hairs will he have?

e. What is the maximum number of white hairs he can grow using this method?

f. If he initially plucks out 26 white hairs, how many hairs will he have in total?

g. Is it possible for him to have an odd number of white hairs on his head?   Y/N

15.

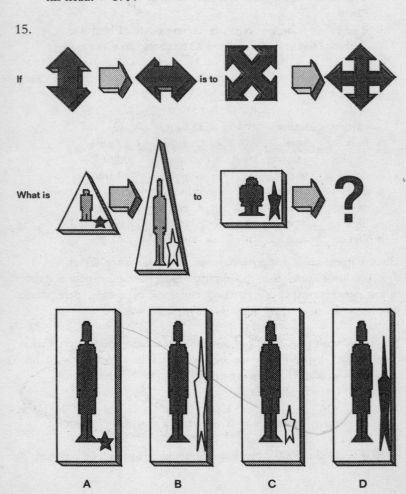

A   B   C   D

16. Insert the missing numbers:

7	7.5		10.5	
14		17	21	29
5		8	3	

17. Label the following diagram with the appropriate letters (a–j):
Example: Where T intersects with O is marked with an arrow.

   a. Where P intersects with Q & S.
   b. Where U intersects with P but not with S.
   c. Where P intersects with U & S but not with Q.
   d. Where S intersects with Q but not with O, P or R.
   e. Where Q intersects with O, R & S, but not with P.
   f. Where S intersects with O & R but not with Q or P.
   g. Where O intersects with S & Q but not with R.
   h. Where O intersects with S & T but not with R or Q.
   i. Where S intersects with P & Q but not with O, R or T.
   j. Where P intersects with S but not with U or Q.

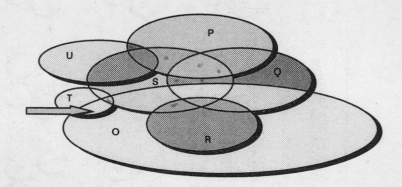

18. Select the word from those in brackets that most closely matches the meaning of the first word.

    a. check (decide, organize, compare, annoy, choose)
    b. impinge (interrupt, suspend, invade, separate, creep)
    c. inextricably (unfathomable, inseparably, sticky, certainly)
    d. bovine (quick, bearish, jocular, smelly, stolid)
    e. swingeing (drastic, mean, oscillating, swelling, lunging)
    f. circuitous (funny, revolution, devious, direct, circular)
    g. lucidity (obscurity, intelligence, hallucinatory, clarity, precision)
    h. genre (genius, select, genuine, sort, individual)
    i. novel (untrue, weird, usual, familiar, fresh)
    j. pander (trouble, satisfy, surprise, whim, enthuse)
    k. overt (open, organize, crude, sworn, magnify)
    l. benign (sweet, harmless, cancer, tumour, deadly)

19. Insert the missing numbers.

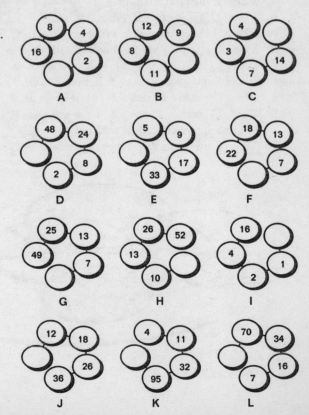

20. In each set below, which is the odd one out?

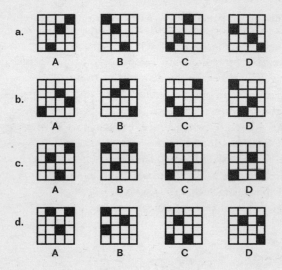

SCORING

The answers are on pages 136–7. Mark your points below:

1.	___	11.	___
2.	___	12.	___
3.	___	13.	___
4.	___	14.	___
5.	___	15.	___
6.	___	16.	___
7.	___	17.	___
8.	___	18.	___
9.	___	19.	___
10.	___	20.	___
		Total	___

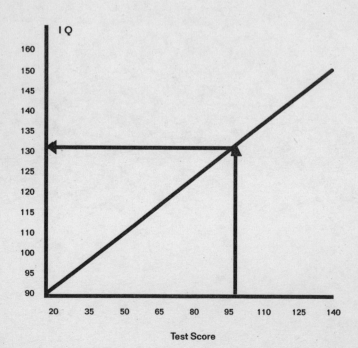

To convert your total score to IQ points, read along the score line until you reach the mark you achieved, draw a line up to meet the diagonal line and draw a line along to determine your IQ. In the example shown, a score of 102 gives an IQ of about 130, + or − 5 points. If you managed to score over 135 before converting to IQ points in much less than the time permitted, your score can be roughly extrapolated by multiplying by 60 and dividing by the number of minutes taken to complete the test.

If your IQ works out to be over 130 on this test you may be eligible for membership of one of the 'high IQ' organizations.

There is a second IQ test on pages 123–135. Before you attempt it, work through the practice tests. Then compare your scores.

Preparing for Tests

• •

Ten or more points can be added to anyone's IQ score by emotional and mental preparation and by being in the right frame of mind during the test. If you are just taking a test for the fun of challenging yourself, those extra points may not matter much, but if you are sitting, say, a college entrance examination, or a selection test for entry to a higher grade at work, those extra points could make the difference between success and failure.

Even with sophisticated testing procedures our personal IQ scores can vary from one day to the next. Many factors influence how well we perform, and by becoming aware of these factors, we can not only improve our IQ scores but can perform better in any test or at any task that requires brain power.

We each have a personal body-clock that determines our peak performance times. Most of us take some time to get going after getting up in the morning, and slow down again for a while after lunch and by the end of the working day. For those who work from nine to five, peak performance is usually between 10am and 12 noon, and between 2.30 and 4.00pm. Thus, the best time to arrange IQ tests, examinations or other mental tasks, is at the beginning of our peak performance times. If you work different hours, you are probably aware of the times of day when you are most alert. Of course, it is not always possible to arrange tests for our own convenience, and then it is necessary to adjust our body-clock as much as possible beforehand, in the same way that we can compensate for jet-lag after travelling between different time zones.

A healthy body helps to produce a healthy mind. Studies at Manchester University have shown that being super-fit can increase our mental capacities, while those who are unfit can be affected by as much as 20 per cent. Fitness also enables us to retain our peak intelligence later in life, letting 70 year olds think as well as 50 year olds. To be able to think at our best we need to be fit. Our brain is the greediest user of oxygen in our body, using 20 per cent of all the oxygen we take in. Aerobic exercise can help to ensure the supply of oxygen that our brain needs, by teaching our blood to use oxygen more efficiently, by increasing the size of blood vessels throughout our body and by getting our heart to pump more oxygenated blood to our brain. Before you go into the test or examination room, if you're fit enough, go for a short run to get your heart pumping a bit faster. Warning: always consult your doctor before beginning a new exercise regime.

What we eat affects the way we think. For most people a high-carbohydrate/low-protein breakfast is best. For lunch, include a food with medium protein, such as low-fat cheese. Do not eat too much before a test, or your body and mind will switch to 'rest and digest' mode, and your pituitary gland will start releasing hormones to make you sleepy. Whatever you do, don't take a 'liquid lunch' before doing a test. In fact, it is better to totally abstain from alcohol and other unnecessary drugs for at least a week before you need to use your head at its best.

Because the urge to smoke causes reduced concentration and that urge is impossible to satisfy in some test situations, it is better to remove the urge entirely by giving up smoking. Do give yourself enough time to recover from withdrawal symptoms, as they can be equally distracting.

Many people find that they can think clearer when taking a regular supply of vitamins A, B complex, C and E, and a multi-mineral and multi-vitamin supplement. Ginseng, the Chinese root, is another supplement that some people find has a beneficial effect on their alertness. In your normal daily diet try to get as much fresh fruit and vegetables as possible, and cut out animal fats and other blood-vessel damaging fats. It may not be merely coincidence that many of the greatest thinkers in the world, including Archimedes, Leonardo da Vinci, Galileo Galilei, Isaac Newton, Benjamin Franklin and Albert Einstein, were vegetarians.

Fifteen minutes before commencing a test, eat an athlete's energy-producing 'powerbar', which are available from sports shops and health-food shops. Also take another unwrapped bar in to eat half-way through the test. Mental work is energy draining, and the brain requires food to burn. Immediately before the test take a hot drink like coffee, chocolate, or tea, preferably with sugar. You may be able to take a drink in with you, in which case choose a glucose-rich drink.

Studies have shown that listening to complex music for 20 minutes before a test can temporarily increase the IQ score by as much as 15 points. It appears that the music stimulates the same parts of the brain that are used for problem solving, and the music acts as a sort of mental limbering-up exercise. Many people find that listening to Beethoven or Vivaldi for 20 minutes before the test is effective. Long-term effects have not been proven, but it seems likely that some residual effect should occur from the regular use of music in this way. When the brain is stimulated by any type of information over an extended period, it undergoes physical effects that help us to process that information. Thus we gain skill and expertise at any task we repeatedly tackle.

It can take a while to get into your rhythm. Do some test examples immediately before your test, to get in the mood. Try to do them as fast as possible, using full concentration. Take advantage of any rest periods offered by the invigilator to rest your eyes and relax for a while. Our performance tends to start dropping after 30 minutes of mentally taxing work, but after a two- or three-minute break it returns to peak.

Test sessions vary as do the environments in which they are held. It may even be possible to arrange an individual test. If you are with a group, try to get a good seat, the closer to the front the better. Don't sit by a window, where outside events may distract you. Also, don't sit directly by a radiator, where you may get too warm, or by a door where you may be disturbed by late-comers or toilet-goers.

If something is wrong with the environment in the test room, tell the invigilator before the test begins. A flapping window blind or a shaky chair can be a distraction that costs points. It is better, if you have the choice to alter the room temperature, to be comfortably cool rather than comfortably warm. Heat tends to make us drowsy.

If you feel unwell, stop writing and tell the examiner. You will be able to resit the test at a later date, which is infinitely preferable to struggling on and scoring below your best.

Stay focused. Loss of focus is a thief of test time.

Study practice

Since man first walked on earth, every generation has built on the work of those who went before. We learnt how to make sharper flints and better spears; how to tame and then to make fire; how to make crude and then more efficient animal traps – and so on, down the ages, from the bow and arrow to the microchip. Totally new concepts seldom occur. The most modern computers have a family tree that goes back to knotted string. No discoveries of enduring value have been made in total isolation from the living tradition of knowledge. Even the giant leaps of imagination and knowledge by Galileo, Newton, Faraday, Pasteur, Bell and Marconi were built on foundations laid by others. Galileo studied Archimedes and Copernicus; Newton studied Euclid, Galileo and Decartes; Bell studied Volta, Grey and Edison. If they had had to start from scratch, it is unlikely that any of them would have achieved what they did.

By emulating these men of genius, and by learning from those who have gone before, we can enhance our lives and tap into an endless source of ideas and inspiration. The sum of human knowledge is now more available than ever before. We all have access to libraries that Galileo could only dream of and to computer power that was impossible only a few years ago.

The ability to find things out is an important skill in our information-hungry world and can even be considered an aspect of intelligence. If you can find knowledge that your neighbour cannot, or if you are faster and more thorough at finding things out, you are clearly more adept than your neighbour at the acquisition of knowledge, and that can make all the difference to your job, your life and your IQ.

Although technology sometimes gets in the way of knowledge – you can waste hours struggling through an electronic memo to find things that should be stored in your head – it makes sense to take advantage of technology whenever you can, and it can often be unavoidable. The microfiche and computer indexing systems in libraries, for example, are valuable aids to study and are not difficult to get the hang of. If you really want to challenge technology, take a computing course at your local technical college. In the words of Samuel Johnson: 'Knowledge is of two kinds. We know a subject ourselves, or we know where we can find information on it.' Further, because no information exists in isolation, you are certain to discover a lot more than you need – when you look for one thing, you can discover another.

If, for example, you have to solve a problem involving speed, it will help if you have previously studied the relationship between speed, distance and time. Or if you are looking up the names of the planets, you may discover the laws of inverse proportion and gain a basic insight into the nature of gravity. Then, if you are asked a question about thrown or falling objects, your knowledge of the subject may help to enhance your common sense. Similarly, if you have to solve a visual-spatial problem, a good basic knowledge of geometry will help your mind to wrap around the shapes involved.

More importantly, it is during the lone quest for true knowledge that all great discoveries, and every advance in human thought have come about.

Albert Einstein said: 'The only thing we can be certain of in this life is that we can be certain of nothing.' Francis Bacon said: 'If a man will begin with certainties, he shall end in doubts; but if he be content to begin with doubts, he shall end in certainties.'

They had different approaches, but both believed in the spirit of enquiry. Thus the ability to ask 'Why?' 'How do you know that?' 'Can you prove that?' 'Let me see the evidence.' and 'How can I find out more?' is an essential attribute of the thinker.

Writing is to reading, as thinking is to doing. It is possible to read a book carefully and yet within a week or two to be left with only a vague memory of what it was about. Reading is a passive activity if all you do is allow the words to pass through your mind. In fact, most people who read at normal speed retain in the long term only about one-tenth of what they have read, and even a few minutes after reading a single page the average reader has difficulty recalling the main subjects of that page. If you doubt that, try to recall the details of the previous page or two that you have just read. See also the next section on speed reading.

The following suggestions are based on my own study methods. I have found that if you accumulate even a small amount of knowledge on a regular basis you can be rich in comparison to others.

- Read in an interactive way. Take an active part in every book you read. If it is your own book, use a highlighter pen to mark any passages that interest you. Write notes in the margins. Insert page-marking tabs, made from self-adhesive labels, so that you can turn directly to the passages that interest you.

- Read in a discriminating way. Never take anything at face value. Authors' opinions differ, and therefore some of those opinions will be right and some will be wrong. In addition, some authors state opinions as facts or fail to check the facts they offer as truth. Even Aristotle, the 'father of logical thought', was prone to making assumptions without proof. He stated, for example, that men have more teeth than women, and despite being married twice he never asked one of his wives to open her mouth to let him count her teeth. If he had done so he would have discovered that he was wrong.

- Read in an investigative way. Look up names referred to in the text to find out more about them. Tracking down references can be both great fun and informative. If you read a quote by someone, it is almost certain that the same person said or wrote many more words of wisdom.

- Write a synopsis. At the end of every chapter write a short summary of that chapter in a notebook or in the chapter-end spaces, both by using your memory and by referring back to the text. This will have the immediate effect of focusing your mind on what you read as you read it, in the knowledge that you will soon have to write about it. It will also change your mode of learning from passive to active. The bonus will be that you will always have the summaries to remind you of the main points of the book.

That last point is probably the most important learning tool. You'll find that most subjects can be reduced to a few essentials that are easy to memorize. This chapter, for example, could be summarized as:

- Use our heritage of knowledge
- Gain investigative skill
- Use technology
- Learn to gain insight
- Discover the truth for yourself
- Read: interact, discriminate, investigate, summarize

To achieve concision it is often necessary to sacrifice richness of material, but because the act of summarizing is a process that happens as you read rather than after you have read, the new, active mode of learning ensures that far more material is absorbed than would otherwise be the case.

Speed Reading

The principle of concise summary is one of the arts behind speed reading. By concentrating on essentials and learning to ignore non-essentials, we can retain more of the material we read. Thus we get the best of both worlds – not only can we read faster but we learn more at the same time. That seems to be a contradiction, but everyone who learns to speed read proves otherwise. After some practice at speed-reading, most people can, on average, read four books in the time it previously took them to read one, with considerably improved long-term retention.

If you work in an office you probably spend at least an hour a day reading mail, reports and proposals. Decisions cannot be made until you have read the information on which those decisions will be based. Only then can you decide what is important and what can be ignored. If you are a student you may spend hours every day reading, but real learning doesn't usually begin until you have summarized the material you are studying.

Perhaps you already consider yourself to be a fast reader. Time yourself while you read the following 500-word passage at your normal speed.

THE RANDOM ELEMENT
Definition: Random – without aim, direction, rule or method. Synonyms : Chance, stray, casual, fortuitous, accidental, haphazard. The introduction of a random element into any particular situation is liable to change the situation in unpredictable ways. In 1866, Alfred Nobel, the Swedish pioneer of nitro-glycerine, had a problem with the transportation of that volatile liquid. Ships were refusing to carry it after 70 cases blew up a ship docked in Panama. Sixty people were killed, buildings on shore were wrecked, and another ship was badly damaged.

Nobel had a difficult problem to solve. The explosive liquid had already claimed his young brother, a number of his friends and his factory in Norway. A few days later it destroyed a block of buildings in San Francisco, killing another 15 people. Alfred had already spent many years trying to tame the liquid, but his experiments were mainly concerned with how to make it less dangerous. Were it not for a random element entering the equation, it is likely that he would never have found the solution, and the use of nitro-glycerine as an explosive would have been abandoned.

One day, as Nobel was inspecting a load, he happened to notice that a temporary packaging material called Kieselguhr (a light German soil) readily soaked up spilled nitro-glycerine. When Alfred took some away and tested it, he discovered that a mixture of three parts nitro-glycerine and one part Kieselguhr made a stable explosive, which he named dynamite. This new explosive quickly made him a millionaire, enabling him to leave, at the end of his long life, the equivalent of two million British pounds (in today's terms at least a hundred times that amount), to fund the Nobel Prizes. Despite his passion for explosives, Nobel was a great pacifist.

Had Nobel known the principles of random association, it is possible that he would have solved his problem much sooner, but we must give him credit for being able to use the event when it did occur. It is clear that he must have said, 'What if...?' many times before the final solution presented itself. If Nobel had not been in an appropriately aware state of mind, the potential of Kieselguhr would have been overlooked.

This is something that we find repeatedly. People do not simply wake up one day with the solutions to problems with which they have never been associated. Apples land on a lot of heads, but they don't all cause whoever happened to be under the trees to come up with amazing new theories of gravity. Only those who have studied mathematics, astronomy and physics and those who are dissatisfied with current explanations and are actively seeking new explanations, are liable to come up with such alternatives. Newton was in the correct state of mind to say, 'What if the force that dropped this apple is the same force that attracts us to the planet and the same force that allows our planet to continue to circle the sun without spinning off into space? What if I am right, and everybody else in the world is wrong?'

The average reading speed for the general population is around 250 words a minute, so if you took longer than two minutes to read that passage, you currently read at less than average speed. If you managed it in less than two minutes, you read faster than average. Whatever your reading speed, you may be interested to know that those who have mastered the techniques of speed reading manage an average of 1,000 words a minute, with some experts managing many times that. Even at the minimum, a speed reader quarters the time taken to read anything.

Answer the following questions to check how well you have retained the passage you have just read. If you want to check your long-term retention after one read, leave these questions for a few days before attempting them.

a. What was the title of the article?
b. What year was mentioned?
c. What was Nobel's nationality?
d. Where was the ship that blew up docked?
e. How many were killed when the ship blew up?
f. Where was Nobel's factory?
g. Where was the block of buildings that blew up?
h. What was the name of the light German soil?
i. How did Nobel discover it?
j. What was the question Newton was in the correct state of mind to ask?

The answers are at the foot of this page.

If you scored over three for short-term retention, you did better than average. If you scored over six, you did very well. If you scored between eight and ten, you have exceptional retention. Try coming back to the question later, after you have had some practice with the techniques of speed reading. You will almost certainly do much better.

Normal reading is not, as a rule, a good way of planting information in our memories for keeps. The techniques of rapid reading, on the other hand, are far better at planting information in there for keeps. The method that follows is simple to describe and not difficult to put into practice, but like any other skill, it does take the three Ds – Desire, Discipline and Dedication. Master each step before you move on to the next. You didn't learn to read in a day so it must be worth a few hours' study and practice for something that will save you time every day for the rest of your life.

FIVE STEPS TO SPEED READING

1. *Try* to read faster. Simply by trying, most people can double their speed. This requires a simple reminder on a regular basis until the habit is instilled. Put up a large card with the words 'speed read', or simply S R, in a place where it will act as a reminder.

2. Try not to sub-vocalize the words as you read them. This sounds difficult, but it can be mastered by most people with a few hours' practice. It is similar to when a child learns not to read aloud.

3. Instead of reading words individually, use only two eye movements per line. Break lines into two and focus on the centre of each half of the line at a time. Try the method with the following quotation by Benjamin Franklin.

There are two ways of being happy, – we means – either will do – the result is the himself, and to do that which happens to however hard it may be to diminish your If you are active and prosperous, or young, augment your means than to diminish your the same time, young or old, rich or poor, do both in such a way as to augment the may either diminish our wants, or augment our same; and it is for each man to decide for be the easiest. If you are idle, or sick, or poor, wants, it will be harder to augment your means. or in good health, it may be easier for you to wants. But if you are wise, you will do both at sick or well ; and if you are very wise, you will general happiness of society.

4. Now try to do the same, but split each line into two halves yourself by flicking your eyes from side to side in two definite steps:

There are two ways of being happy, – we may either diminish our wants, or augment our means – either will do – the result is the same; and it is for each man to decide for himself, and to do that which happens to be the easiest. If you are idle, or sick, or poor, however hard it may be to diminish your wants, it will be harder to augment your means. If you are active and prosperous, or young, or in good health, it may be easier for you to augment your means than to diminish your wants. But if you are wise, you will do both at the same time, young or old, rich or poor, sick or well ; and if you are very wise, you will do both in such a way as to augment the general happiness of society.

5. Now read the passage that follows, but in each half of the lines, concentrate on the highlighted words. Don't ignore the unhighlighted words, but just be aware as you read that they are less important. If you can manage, try to take in a whole line at a time. Holding the book further away than normal allows you a wider field of vision.

There are **two ways** of being **happy**, – we may either **diminish** our **wants**, or **augment** our **means – either will do** – the **result** is the **same**; and it is for **each man** to **decide** for himself, and to **do** that which happens to be the **easiest**. **If** you are **idle**, or **sick**, or **poor**, however **hard** it may be **to diminish** your **wants**, it will be **harder to augment** your **means**. **If** you are **active** and **prosperous**, or **young**, or in **good health**, it may be **easier** for you to **augment** your **means than** to **diminish** your **wants**. But **if** you are **wise**, you **will**

do both at the same time, young or old, rich or poor, sick or well ; and **if** you are **very wise**, you will **do both** in such a way as **to augment** the general **happiness of society**.

(This illustrates Benjamin Franklin's outlook on life, which could be summarized as: work harder or cut costs, but serve society.)

Speed progression from this point is a matter of ongoing practice. You will gradually develop the ability, while glancing briefly once at each paragraph, to pick out the key words, and follow their meanings and implications. When the subject is difficult and contains a lot of complex concepts, speed reading is harder to achieve with good comprehension, but practice brings increased proficiency. If necessary, use a bookmark or your index finger to help pull your eyes down the page. You'll be able to force your eyes to follow the fast-moving marker after a bit of practice.

If you read something once, when you know you are going to have to read it again, highlight the areas of interest. Underlining or circling with a pen does the trick if you don't have a highlighter handy at any time. When you pick it up again, you'll be able to go straight to the relevant passages.

If you forget most of the above, remember the first principle of speed reading – that the simple act of trying to read faster is one of the most effective ways to develop that skill.

Verbal and Linguistic Ability

The ability to express our thoughts and ideas and to understand what is being communicated to us is clearly of great importance. If we have only a limited understanding of our own first language, we miss a lot of what goes on and are forced to live at a lower level of awareness and existence. Employers understand this very well, and many industrial psychologists design aptitude tests with a high verbal content. If two prospective employees have the same qualifications and all other things are equal, the more articulate job-seeker will be chosen, and if IQ tests are used in the selection process, verbal/linguistic performance may be given a high priority The same is true when it comes to promotion – an articulate answer to a question from the selection board can make the vital difference.

When we sit down to take an IQ test, there is nowhere to hide. We cannot pretend we have abilities that we do not possess. If there are words we don't know, that will be exposed, and no matter how intelligent we may be in other areas, our score will be pulled down.

The best three tips for gaining a wide vocabulary, and helping your overall IQ score are:

- Read widely on every subject possible.
- Never pass a word you do not understand without: looking it up in a dictionary, memorizing it, learning how to spell it, writing it fifty times, absorbing it into your vocabulary and using it regularly from now on.
- Never stop learning. Make learning a hobby and an obsession.

It pays to concentrate on spelling if you have a weakness in this area. Poor spellers tend to use similar sounding words in the wrong way. They also read and write more slowly and are consequently slower at doing verbal/linguistic problems. Worse than that, to those who can spell some spelling mistakes can appear funny or ridiculous or both.

The following practice problems, games and puzzles are designed to boost your verbal/linguistic ability while you are having fun doing them. Some of the problems contain words that are often misunderstood and misused, so do use a dictionary when necessary, but don't let it take the place of your brain.

No time limit has been set on the practice sessions, but try to complete them as quickly as you can. If you prefer to spread your practice over an extended period, it is more valuable to do a little every day than a lot every few weeks.

For best results, read through all the questions before you begin and do not look at the answers until you have done your best. Remember that you will always retain information better if you discover it for yourself through investigation, study, and sheer hard work.

Practice Test

1. Check the spelling of the following words. Tick those that are correct and write the correct spelling of those that are wrong.

a. orstrasise _____

b. genesis _____

c. fearfull _____

d. exitement _____

e. exeedingly _____

f. sustenence _____

g. silouette _____

h. divertion _____

i. soulless _____

j. reminiscence _____

k. effluent _____

l. happenning _____

m. formidible _____

n. pretentious _____

o. regrettable _____

2. Solve the clues to complete the word grid.

Vertical clue (column 2): use to row

Vertical clue (column 4): jockeys need

large stoned fruit	p		a		h
famous American battle			a		
bird/man/fish			v		
Norsemen			n		
contract			a		
flavour of time	e		h		s

3. Insert the number of letters indicated by the dashes to create seven valid words.

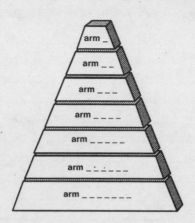

arm _
arm _ _
arm _ _ _
arm _ _ _ _
arm _ _ _ _ _
arm _ _ _ _ _ _
arm _ _ _ _ _ _ _

4. Match the people below with the following quotes.

   a. Remember, that time is money.
   b. If you would hit the mark, you must aim a little above it;
     Every arrow that flies feels the attraction of earth.
   c. Though I am always in haste, I am never in a hurry.
   d. Our greatest glory consists not in never falling, but in rising
     every time we fall.
   e. Let me smile with the wise and feed with the rich.
   f. I came, I saw, I conquered.

Frederick the Great, Henry Wadsworth Longfellow, Samuel Johnson, Julius Caesar, John Wesley, Benjamin Franklin, Oliver Goldsmith

5. Find the missing words, selecting from the list below. Example: lick, <u>mouth</u>, suck.

   a. touch, _____, stroke

   b. see, _____, cry

   c. kick, _____, walk

   d. write, _____, draw

   e. dig, _____, bury

   f. read, _____, learn

   g. enter, _____, exit

   h. hunt, _____, shoot

Choose from: hole, scribe, purchase, road, eyes, release, throw, feet, drop, pencil, hand, expire, look, rifle, run, spade, grasp, book, room, acquire, sell, sad, door, sensual, art

6. Underline the odd one out. Example: car, automobile, vehicle, motor, buggy, <u>Jaguar</u>.

   a. swear, assert, avow, curse, testify, declare
   b. prove, authenticate, decide, confirm, justify, verify
   c. provoke, irritate, enrage, irk, precipitate, incense
   d. narrow, slender, tight, restricted, limited, scarce
   e. judge, appraise, convict, assess, estimate, examine

7. Find the seven hidden words in this grid to reveal an aspect of brain power in the shaded column:

press on ink	p			
containers for liquid	t			
dilute	w			
become this with practice	a			
not nearly	f			
religious diversifications	c			
augment	s			
phase	c			
inexorable	f			

8. The following words are often misunderstood. A definition has been given next to each one. Identify the correct and incorrect definitions.

a. Eldorado: a place of opportunity and wealth
b. Influx: electromagnetic energy field
c. Contumacious: ignorant and rude
d. Isotropic: having uniform physical properties
e. Telegenic: of pleasant appearance
f. Non-aligned: broken
g. Opaque: totally impenetrable to light
h. Theorem: a proposition that can never be proven
i. Peerless: beyond all doubt
j. Hyperbole: exaggeration
k. Sylvan: smooth as silk
l. Obdurate: hard-hearted
m. Specious: extra special
n. Gauche: tactless
o. Concomitant: accompanying
p. Antipathy: confirmed dislike towards
q. Secular: belonging to a particular religious order
r. Insolate: protect from sunlight
s. Delimit: to remove the limits of

t. Volition: the act of choosing or willing
u. Cognate: easily understood
v. Kappa: a scullcap worn by those of the Jewish faith
w. Insouciance: a couldn't-care-less attitude
x. Laity: those of a profession such as clergy, law or medicine
y. Solecism: a word giving solace to others
z. Inflection: a change in the tone of voice

9. In each of the following , underline the two words that are opposite in meaning. Example: <u>abuse</u>, mock, lampoon, <u>honour</u>, comfort.

a. memorable, special, important, ordinary, usual
b. angry, desolate, forlorn, cheerful, emotional
c. genuine, real, wrong, artificial, sham
d. propel, oblige, dissuade, compel, deter
e. immaculate, faulty, spoiled, contaminated, clean
f. drooping, floppy, flabby, strong, firm
g. horizontal, bumpy, flat, rough, plane
h. lower, appreciate, inflate, decrease, depreciate
i. clutch, return, snatch, seize, release
j. muddy, dirty, hazy, clean, clear
k. mysterious, understandable, strange, weird, perplexing

10. In each of the following underline the word that is the odd one out. Example: blue, <u>colour</u>, pink, green, red.

a. begin, start, commence, immediately, proceed
b. morning, suppertime, evening, noon, afternoon
c. look, see, observe, find, scrutinize
d. confine, imprison, detain, trap, incarcerate
e. jumpy, nervous, cowardly, fearful, worried
f. pure, undefiled, sterile, unmixed, unsullied
g. indefinitely, eternal, everlasting, perpetual, unchanging
h. fight, attack, seize, engage, tackle
i. pester, trick, harass, provoke, annoy
j. caress, touch, feel, handle, hold
k. joyful, content, buoyant, cheerful, happy
l. forgery, copy, duplicate, facsimile, replica

11. Test your logic by completing the following sentences by two famous authors. Select the words from the lists below. Although several words may fit, only the correct words will give the quotations their true sense and flavour.

a. True _____ is of a retired _____, and an enemy to pomp and noise. It _____, in the first place, from the _____ of one's self, and, in the _____, from the _____ and conversation of a _____ select _____.

Joseph Addison

enjoyment, majesty, friendship, few, thousand, happiness, next, last, nature, companions, arises, affairs.

b. Sublime is the _____ of the mind over the _____, that for a time, can make _____ and nerve _____, and string the sinews like _____, so that the _____ become so mighty.

Harriet Beecher Stowe

lead, copper, concentration, steel, flesh, great, height, dominion, cowards, body, weak, impregnable, invisible.

12. Solve the word square to find a word related to brainpower in one of the vertical columns.

to surpass	e			e	
lacking ready cash					e
as thick as a brick		e			e
ransack					e
undiplomatic			u		
troublesome animals		e			
Venus does this backwards			i		
strangle					e
countries		a			

13. Insert the missing words, choosing from the list of words immediately below each sentence.

a. Determine _____ what you are _____ to do in _____ for the _____ you _____ . You _____ get _____ for _____ in _____ life.

going, anything, words, thus, doing, exactly, absolutely, not, thinking, this, nothing, return, things, desire, don't, money, every, whatever, replacement.

b. The _____ goal in _____ must be the _____ of _____ _____ and _____ of _____ . _____ for _____ !

unique, considered, peace, fact, personal, consideration, mind, go, control, happiness, wealth, ultimate, life, it, acquisition, compulsive.

c. Among the most _____ people in _____, the one _____ that _____ of them _____ in common is _____ . Without that, _____ is _____ . With it, _____ is possible.

anything, talented, industry, success, Mexico, thread, successful, quality, flying, nothing, persistence, lucky, little, possible, others, most, have.

d. Within every _____ person is a _____ person _____ to get out. Look deep _____ your _____ being for the _____ and _____ of life that you were _____ with. It's _____ there _____ for _____ .

waiting, confused, happy, crazy, within, thinking, happiness, born, down, equal, still, inner, lurking, you, unhappy, deep, human, time, joy, time, waiting.

e. If you _____ yet _____ _____ goals _____ life, then _____ are _____ to _____ any of _____ . You _____ plan for _____ you _____ yet know you _____ .

your, haven't, want, made, interest, throughout, whom, established, need, must, don't, consider, in, should, answer, you, achieve, can't, them, what, unlikely.

14. Underline the word inside the brackets that is most nearly opposite in meaning to the word outside the brackets. Example: healthy (dying, ill, upset, dizzy, virus).

    a. calm (feverish, frenzied, angry, upset, mad)
    b. shrivelled (bloated, dilated, swollen, inflated, imploded)
    c. deprecate (increase, crow, exaggerate, brag, pride)
    d. transform (commute, change, preserve, mutate, transmit)
    e. termination (birth, beginning, dawn, original, opening)
    f. expose (decide, hidden, withdrawn, impose, cover)
    g. thwart, (compare, contradict, favour, resist, fight)
    h. solid (diluted, watery, fluid, flowing, dripping)
    i. arbitrary (decidedly, confused, reasoned, orderly, efficient)
    j. responsive (cool, concerned, callous, calm, uncaring)

15. Find the prefixes that, when placed before each of the following groups of letters, will create valid words. Each set of words has a different prefix. Example: –ave, –ver, –rgy, become cleave, cleaver, clergy with the prefix cle–.

  a. –ot, –amist, –ht, –wig, –ger, –horn
  b. –bean, –fly, –cup, –milk, –nut, –fat
  c. –ral, –ritis, –ron, –ter, –tron, –tral
  d. –age, –s, –ter, –ening, –ly, –en
  e. –lin, –let, –lence, –la, –lation, –lent

16. Solve this acrossword puzzle to find, in the shaded column, a word that can make all the difference in a relationship.

gaping mouth	r	i	c	t	u	s
redder than pink		l				
eventful end			n			
not harsh colour				t		
brand					m	
not massive						t
to make or form					t	
fail to recall				g		
not entirely clear			a			
shake and hear		a				
inanimate legs	t					
shove through the air		r				
from bad to worse			n			

17. Poetry is a wonderful builder of word power. Find 10 words to rhyme with each of the following:

  a. hair
  b. flake
  c. waiter
  d. tail
  e. drive
  f. stumble
  g. aired

18. Underline the odd word out in each group:

   a. woman, female, girl, she, lady
   b. string, rope, thread, gut, shoelace
   c. free, impartial, autonomous, enduring, independent
   d. incurable, invertebrate, hopeless, untreatable, incorrigible
   e. fly, soar, zoom, glide, flit

19. Sort these animal classifications into their correct pairs:

   dog – vulpine
   wolf – canine
   fox – lupine
   cow – piscine
   bear – bovine
   fish – ursine

20. Decode the following to find a valuable insight into knowledge from Dr Samuel Johnson (1709–84), the famous lexicographer, writer, conversationalist and wit.

Clue: QUERTY keyboard layout   QWERTYUIOP
                                  ASDFGHJKL
                                  ZXCVBNM

Szz lmpezrfhr od oydrzg pg dpqr bszir. Yjrtr od mpyjomh dp qomiyr pt omvpmdofrtsnzr, yjsy o epizf mpy tsyjrt lmpe oy yjsm mpy.

21. Complete the following proverbs:

   a. Give him an inch …
   b. The devil finds work …
   c. A friend to everybody …
   d. Experience is the mother of …
   e. Don't teach your grandmother …
   f. What the eye doesn't see …
   g. To have a friend …
   h. Faint heart …
   i. It is better to be a live coward …

j. Where there's muck ...
k. Power tends to corrupt ...
l. Brevity is ...
m. High fences ...
n. There's many a slip ...
o. Nothing succeeds ...
p. All is fair ...
q. There's no fool ...
r. Those who can, do ...
s. If you want something done ...
t. Never leave a highway ...
u. Winners never quit ...
v. A tree often transplanted ...
w. It is better to be a hammer ...
x. The misfortunes hardest to bear ...
y. A nod is as good as a wink ...
z. Marry in haste ...

22. Insert the missing words in the following sentence, from the words in brackets.

To have a friend who is always _____, (masterful, there, faithful)

never _____, always pleased to see you, (naughty, kind, angry, gone)

never _____, ever loving, and who would (deceitful, proud, loving, wild)

give his or her life to _____ you, you must (find, see, share, protect, love)

either find your _____, or buy a dog. (nemesis, self, dog, soul-mate)

23. A haulage company describes its service in the shaded line in this acrossword puzzle. How good does it claim to be?

a measure of strength			▓		
communication device			▓		
pretty Scot			▓		
not a female parent			▓		
to attempt to persuade			▓		
between Venus and Mars			▓		
draw a conclusion			▓		
peccadillo			▓		
asinine			▓		

24. Correct the spelling of the following words. If you do not already know them, learn what they mean.

a. caligraphy
b. computor
c. penelise
d. emmolient
e. correspondance
f. acheivement
g. percieve
h. managable
i. tactfull
j. harbringer
k. rancourous
l. vigourous
m. ingenousness

n. illiteratly
o. mnenomically
p. rubiayat
q. practicible
r. fiascoes
s. cancerogenic
t. beachcomers
u. flegmatic
v. extragivansa
w. covetosness
x. lieuftenant
y. locomotiv
z. countenence

Scoring

The comments below are intended as a guide only, but if your score is close to a borderline, read the next comments too.

Mark your scores here:

1. _____   2. _____   3. _____

4. _____   5. _____   6. _____

7. _____   8. _____   9. _____

10. _____   11. _____   12. _____

13. _____   14. _____   15. _____

16. _____   17. _____   18. _____

19. _____   20. _____   21. _____

22. _____   23. _____   24. _____

Total _____

Total $\div$ 35.5 $\times$ 10 = percentage score_____

100–80 per cent: Excellent. You have a fine understanding of the language and an aptitude for verbal and linguistic problems. Even so, it is possible to continue improving by expanding your vocabulary and your knowledge through reading and learning.

79–60 per cent: Above average. You clearly have an interest in words and are probably improving your knowledge all the time. With greater application and deeper reading you will gain an even larger vocabulary.

59–40 per cent: Average. You are fairly competent with words, but there is room for improvement. When you come across a word you don't understand, don't pass it by until you have found what it means and you have noted it down for future reference.

Below 40 per cent: Don't be disheartened by your score. Most people misunderstand some words. It is highly unlikely that you read books for recreation, so it would be worth cultivating the habit. Choose light fiction to begin with so that you do not lose interest before finishing. Later, when you have developed the concentration that results from regular reading, you can move to more difficult material.

Numerical Ability

● ●

Numerical IQ questions are not, as a rule, difficult to solve. The calculations involved are quite easy if you can add, subtract, multiply and divide. If you can also manipulate simple fractions and decimals, find percentages and do basic algebra, very few numerical IQ questions should baffle you – provided, of course, that you are able to realize the correct methods of solution from the range of possibilities available.

This chapter provides practice with most types of numerical problems. If you don't manage to solve a problem the first time you meet it, discover where you went wrong and learn the processes involved. The next time you meet a similar problem, you will be better prepared and your mind will be able to use the tracks you have already laid to find the answer.

It is possible to cut down your calculation time by using certain shortcuts. Here are seven of the most useful:

1. Round up or down before you calculate. If, for example, you have to work out the answer to 40×41, simply calculate $40 \times 40 = 1600$ then add 40 to get 1640. Similarly, to add 199 plus 129, it is easier to add $200 + 129$, then to subtract 1 from the answer.

2. Move the decimal point. It is easy to multiply by 10 or divide by 10 (or by any power of 10 such as 100 or 100,000) by moving the decimal point backwards or forwards. For example, $1929 \div 10 = 192.9$. To mutiply by 10, just add a zero.

3. Break calculations into their simplest elements. If you have to work out 15×9, it may be easier to say $10 \times 9 = 90$, $5 \times 9 = 45$, $90 + 45 = 135$.

4. Add the same to each part of the calculation then subtract the total added from the answer. For example, $19 + 29 + 39 = 20 + 30 + 40$ $(-3) = 87$.

5. Convert to an easier calculation. In multiplication, when you do something to one half of the calculation, you must do the opposite to the other half. If you double one, halve the other. For example, 18×3 is the same as 9×6. Again, if you divide one-half by four, multiply the other half by four, as in $32 \times 4 = 8 \times 16 = (8 \times 10) + (8 \times 6) = 128$. Similarly, when you have to calculate multiplications that are above

your memorized table range, you can split them into smaller parts. $18 \times 9 = \text{double } 9 \times 9 = 2 \times 81$, which is simple to do mentally.

6. **Calculate with components.** Numbers are made up from multiples of digits, tens, hundreds and so on, so $186 + 231 = 18$ tens added to 23 tens $= 41$, and $6 + 1 = 7$, so the answer $= 417$.

7. **Memorize results.** In the same way that you can learn tables for multiplication, it is possible to learn to recognize the results of other number calculations on sight. This is a matter of practice, and many people do it without realizing it. Most people don't have to calculate the result of, say, $9 + 13$. They instantly know the answer because they have done it so many times that they remember it. To take this a step further, memorize the results of every addition of two-digit numbers below 100. That will give you a facility with numbers that should be worth a few IQ points.

You will clearly be more adept with numbers if you know your multiplication tables, so it's a good idea to get some practice in. If you really want to gain an advantage, learn the tables up to 12×24.

To calculate percentages, remember that percent means *per hundred*. 10 per cent means 10 hundredths. So 15 per cent means 15 hundredths. It is easy to divide by 100, so you should be able to find any percentage by first finding one hundredth then multiplying by the percentage quantity. For example, find 12% of 60:

1% of $60 = 0.6$ so $12\% = 12 \times 0.6 = 7.2$

Alternatively, you could say 10% of $60 = 6$, and since $1\% = 0.6$, $2\% = 1.2$, therefore $12\% = 6 + 1.2$,which is 7.2.

To multiply fractions, multiply the tops and bottoms of each part together separately. For example, $\frac{1}{5} \times \frac{3}{5} = \frac{3}{25}$.

To divide fractions, invert the first term and treat as multiplication. For example, $\frac{1}{3} \div \frac{1}{2} = \frac{3}{1} \times \frac{1}{2} = \frac{3}{2} = 1\frac{1}{2}$.

To add fractions, find the lowest common denominator and add the upper terms. For example, $\frac{2}{3} + \frac{3}{4} = \frac{8+9}{12} = \frac{17}{12} = 1\frac{5}{12}$ (because $\frac{2}{3} = \frac{8}{12}$ and $\frac{3}{4} = \frac{9}{12}$).

To subtract fractions, find the lowest common denominator and subtract the upper terms. For example, $\frac{1}{2} - \frac{1}{4} = {}^{2\text{-}}\frac{1}{4} = \frac{1}{4}$ (because $\frac{1}{2} = \frac{2}{4}$).

To calculate areas, multiply length × breadth. For example, if you have to calculate the area of a room measuring 4 × 5m:

Area = 4 × 5 = 20m

To calculate volumes, multiply length × breadth × height. For example, to find the volume of a box 4m high, 7m long and 2m wide:

$4 \times 7 \times 2 = 56m^3$ (56 cubic m)

To convert hours to the 24-hour clock, add 12 to any time after noon:

1pm becomes 13.00hrs, and 2pm becomes 14.00hrs and so on.

To convert back from 24-hour clock to a 12-hour clock, deduct 12 from any time after noon: 19.00hrs becomes 7pm and 07.15hrs becomes 7.15am.

To calculate distance, time or speed, use the formula
speed = distance ÷ time which can be converted for use in any part of the equation: distance = speed × time, and time = distance ÷ speed.

Numerical Practice Test 1

1. Insert the missing numbers.

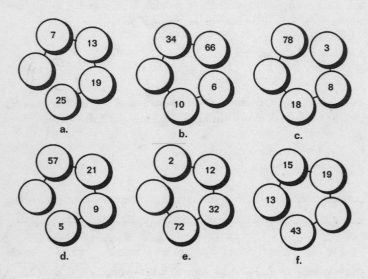

2. A car travels at a constant speed of 40 kph.

   a. How long will it take to cover 30 kilometres?
   b. How many minutes will it take to pass the halfway mark if the destination is 80 kilometres away?
   c. How far will it travel in 12 minutes?
   d. How long will it take the driver to get home from 160 kilometres away?

3. Find the missing number.

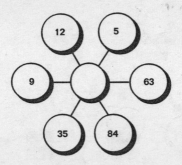

4. Insert the missing numbers in each set.

Example

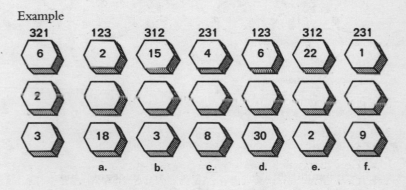

5. If c is 12 to d, and e is 35 to g, what is b to i ?

6. Insert the missing numbers.

   a. 25, 15, 22, 12, X, 9, 16, 6
   b. 3, 0, 6, 3, 9, 6, X, 9
   c. 2, 4, 3, 6, 5, 10, 9, X
   d. 5, 15, 7, 21, 13, 39, X, 93
   e, 4, 20, 5, 25, 10, 50, 35, X

7. Which shape, — A, B, C, D, E or F — should come next?

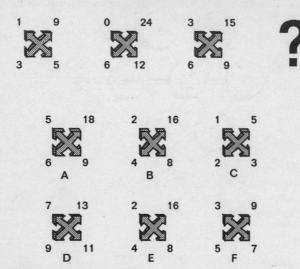

8. Complete the analogy:

   dog is to cat as 5, 16, 8 is to __, __, __

9. Solve the following deductive reasoning problems:

   a. What number divided into 38 gives a remainder of 2 and divided into 48 gives a remainder of 3?
   b. What number added to 4 gives a number that, when multiplied by itself, has a result that, when 4 is added, will give 26 when quartered?
   c. What number when divided by 3 gives a number that, when divided by 3, gives a number that, when added to 11, gives a number that, when 1 is subtracted, gives a number that when divided by 7 gives 3?
   d. What number divided by 5 gives a number that, when multiplied by 3, gives a number that, when added to itself, gives a number that, when divided by 10, gives a number that, when multiplied by itself, gives a number that when multiplied by 9 gives 81?

10. With the weight of the balls as shown, if 16 grey balls are added on the left-hand side, how many black balls will have to be added to the right-hand side to make the scales balance?

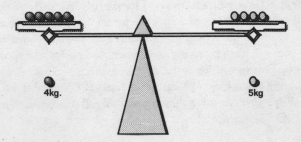

4kg.

5kg

SCORING

If you got more than three of these correct you are better than average at number problems. If you got most of them correct you will achieve a very high score in most numerical IQ tests, provided that you do them fast enough. While you are learning the principles, it is important to attempt as many of the tests as you possibly can. Even if you don't succeed, you will learn by trying, and when you go back to those problems that baffle you, the solution may come.

Bear in mind that most numerical IQ tests are designed to be solved quickly. When you can solve these more difficult problems, you will find most IQ tests easy.

Numerical Practice Test 2

1. Insert the missing number.

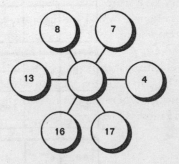

2. A Boeing 747 airliner travelling at 860 kph through calm air normally takes 1½ hours to fly from London to Hanover. Based on this information:
   a. What is the distance from London to Hanover?
   b. How long would it take to get to its destination in a 50 kph headwind?
   c. How long would it take to make a complete return trip with a 36 kph wind blowing in the London to Hanover direction on both legs of the trip?

3. A bank manager is trapped in an airtight safe containing 270 litres of oxygen. Assuming that he dies when all the oxygen is consumed, how long does he live if:

   a. He uses ½ litre with every breath and breathes four times a minute?
   b. He uses ¾ litre with every breath and breathes twice a minute?
   c. He uses ⅓ litre every fifty seconds.
   d. He gets excited, and uses ¼ litre 20 times a minute?

4. Insert the missing numbers.

a.

a10	c 24	e	g 52	i	k 80
b17	d	f 45	h 59	j 73	l

b.

a 10	c	e	g	i 50	k
b	d	f 35	h	j	l 65

c.

a 9	c	e 41	g 57	i	k
b	d 33	f	h	j	l

5. Re-arrange seven numbers in this square so that each horizontal, vertical and diagonal row of five figures totals 21.

1	4	9	5	2
2	9	2	2	9
2	1	4	9	5
4	5	5	1	1
5	4	1	4	9

6. If two apples and three bananas costs 86 credits, and three apples and two bananas costs 74 credits, how much do individual apples and bananas cost?

7. Look at the examples above the squares of figures and apply the patterns to complete the grids.

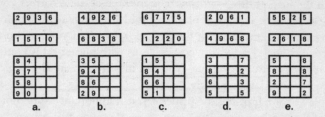

| 2 9 3 6 | 4 9 2 6 | 6 7 7 5 | 2 0 6 1 | 5 5 2 5 |
| 1 5 1 0 | 6 8 3 8 | 1 2 2 0 | 4 9 6 8 | 2 6 1 8 |

8 4	3 5	1 5	3 7	5 8
6 7	9 4	8 4	8 2	8 8
5 8	8 6	6 6	6 3	2 7
9 0	2 9	5 1	5 5	9 2

a.   b.   c.   d.   e.

8. Fill the numbers in the blank circle under grey. Clue: start at F.

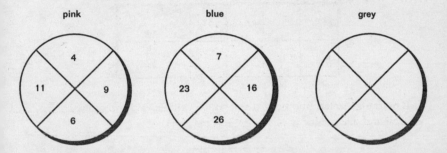

pink   blue   grey

9. Complete the following analogies.
   a. Bad is to good as 25–26–23 is to   _____
   b. Puzzlement is to confusion as 18–23–28 is to   _____
   c. Horatio is to 7–14–17 as Nelson is to   _____

10. David runs a second-hand shop. He sold a radio–cassette at 21.34 credits; a wheel at 19.61 credits; a brass trumpet at 35.82 credits; and a bike at 82.65 credits. When he totalled up his day's takings he found that he only had 147.72 credits instead of the 159.42 credits he expected. David has mistakenly transposed digits. Can you discover where?

SCORING

As with the first set, if you got more than three of these correct you are already better than average at number problems. Your score should improve as you continue with the practice sessions. If you got most of them correct you clearly have no problems with numerical IQ tests, but improvement is always possible. You can improve on an all-correct score by working more quickly.

While you are learning the principles, it is important to attempt as many of the tests as you possibly can. Even if you do not succeed, you will learn by trying, and when you go back to those problems that baffle you, the solution may come. The subconscious often works on problems without the conscious mind being aware of it.

Numerical Practice Test 3

1. Re-arrange eight numbers in this square so that each horizontal, vertical and diagonal row of five figures totals 25.

3	4	3	8	9
3	1	9	1	4
9	9	1	3	8
4	3	8	4	8
8	1	1	4	9

2. Solve the following numerical analogies. Example: 12 is to 18 as 10 is to 15.

   a. 126 is to 252 as 18 is to   _____

   b. 51 is to 17 as 9 is to   _____

   c. 16 is to 128 as 8 is to   _____

   d. 56 is to 8 as 49 is to   _____

   e. 11 is to 22 as 44 is to   _____

   f. 18 is to 324 as 12 is to   _____

3. Insert the missing numbers.

	6		5	4	
7	7	8			9
		11	11	10	

4. Diana opens a book with 225 pages. On the first day she reads 1 page. On the second day she reads 3 pages. On the third day she reads 5 pages and so on until she has finished the book.

   a. How many days does it take her to read the first 100 pages?
   b. How many days does it take her to read the book?
   c. On which day does she read more than twice as many pages as on day 5?
   d. Continuing the reading plan, how many more days would it take her to read the book if it were 400 pages long?

5. If each square is 0.5m × 0.5m and the shaded border is 0.5m all round, find the area of:

   a. The total area covered by black tiles
   b. The shaded border

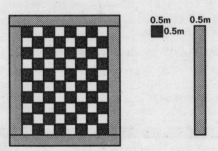

6. Using the numbers 1, 2, 3 and 4 in step-by-step calculations, express the following numbers. Example: $2 = 1 \times 2 \times 3 - 4$.
   a. 23
   b. 36
   c. 11
   d. 0
   e. 3
   f. 9

7. Find the famous date from history:

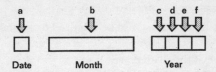

a. The number that is 4 less + 2 than the result of dividing 24 by a sixth of 24.

b. The month that comes four months before the month that comes seven months after April.

c. The number that, when twice multiplied by 8, gives the number that is the result of 2 multiplied by itself 5 times.

d. The number that, when 3 is subtracted and the result multiplied by 4, gives a number which, when both digits are added together, produces 7 as a result.

e. The number that would give the area of one-sixth of the floor space of a room that is 6 units long, 7 units wide and 5.2 units high.

f. The number that has the same value as the number of letters in the name of the only month not beginning with J that has two fewer letters in its name than the value of its position in the calendar.

8. You can fill a 50-litre tub in 2 minutes. When you pull the plug it takes the tub 5 minutes to empty.

a. When empty, how long will it take to refill with the plug left out?

b. With the plug out how long will it take to go from half-full to full?

c. How many litres will be in the tub after 1 minute if the tub has the plug pulled when quarter-full with the tap still running?

9. A policeman is chasing a suspect up a downward escalator of 20 stairs. For every five that he climbs he gets carried down four. How many stairs does he have to climb to get to the top?

10. Calculate:

a. The shaded area
b. The length of fence that would be required to separate area B from area A
c. The perimeter of the shaded area
d. The number of 0.5 × 0.5m tiles required to cover the area of B and C

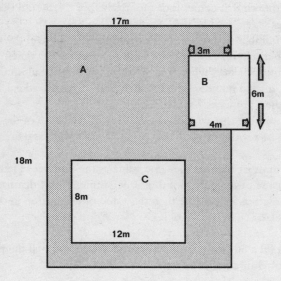

SCORING

Your final score in this set should give you a good idea of your ability to gain expertise at numerical tests, and you should see some improvement in your performance from that of the previous sets. If you haven't yet seen an improvement, keep trying.

Some people have a negative attitude to anything involving numbers, but anyone of normal intelligence can become adept at their use – if they practise. Get hold of maths books that are on the edge of your knowledge limit. Learn to solve just one new type of problem a week, and you'll master over fifty a year. Over a five- to ten-year period, by keeping up revision and continuing the process, you will progress through and beyond school and college maths. In other words, you will develop your numerical IQ to its full potential.

Visual-Spatial Ability

●●

Visual-spatial elements in IQ tests are usually considered a better method of measuring pure intelligence than numerical or verbal-linguistic tests. They tend to be 'culture fair' – in other words, your background, education and knowledge should not affect your score. However, this holds true only for the first time you encounter the tests. Just as practice improves a chess player's ability to visualize moves and strategies or an architect's ability to design buildings, it improves the skill required to complete visual-spatial tasks. As with the other elements of knowledge acquisition, if we can think faster and more accurately about the subject, apply that thinking to the solution of problems and maintain that skill by revision and practice, our intelligence is effectively increased in that area, and our brains change to allow us to access and utilize our new knowledge and skill. If they did not, we would be unable to retain our enhanced abilities over the long term. But changes to the brain are not easily made. For long-term effects to take place we have to put in long-term effort. Knowledge and skill have to be reinforced by revision, and this is particularly true for visual-spatial intelligence, since we are less likely to encounter these problems in everyday life than the linguistic or numerical aspects of IQ testing.

The elements that are measured in visual-spatial tests are observation, depth perception, mental image orientation and logical reasoning. There may also be numerical or verbal-linguistic aspects to the tests. The ability to analyse complex material, to decide what is relevant and to find the key solution elements is not something that can be pigeon-holed. It may take every mental skill you have to solve a particular problem.

Here are ten tips for solving visual-spatial problems (avoid looking at the answers below each puzzle until you have tried to solve the associated problems).

1. Check that the objects are all the same size. Sometimes the most obvious solutions can be overlooked. Pick the odd one out from the following shapes.

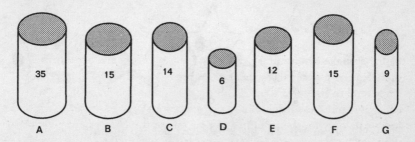

The odd one out is A. The number 35 is clearly too large in relation to the comparative volume of the cylinder.

2. Check for mirror-image or other reversal. This is a common way of creating an odd-one-out problem. Pick the odd one out from the following.

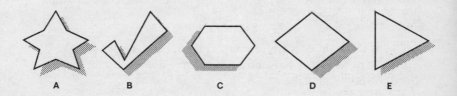

The odd one out is C. It is the only figure with a shadow on the left.

3. Check for patterns in the sequence of objects. What breaks the sequence? Choose the odd one out from the following objects.

A B C D E

The odd one out is E. The black balls have skipped an arm.

4. Check for patterns in internal features within the objects. Choose the odd one out from the following.

A B C D E

The odd one out is A. It is the only shape that does not contain within it a copy of the next shape in the sequence. (Roll over at E.)

5. Count the number of faces, points, corners, bases, shapes or markings, to see if they have a relationship to a number on the shapes. Insert the missing numbers on A, B, C and D below.

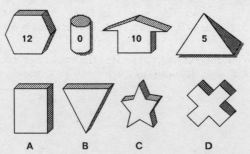

A B C D

A = 8, B = 6, C = 10, D = 16. The number of outside corners on the shapes = the numbers on the shapes . (Inside corners do not count. You can tell this by the number on the arrow.)

6. Check for numerical substitution where each shape represents a number. Try substituting numbers for shapes and adding, subtracting, multiplying or dividing columns or rows with different numbers substituted.

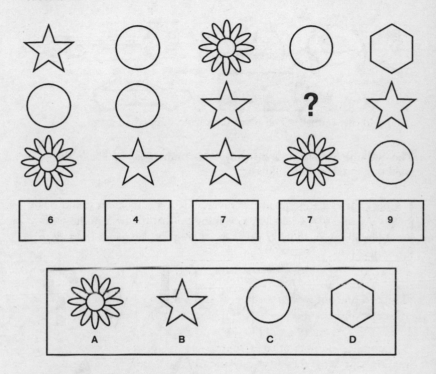

The missing shape is A, the flower, because 3+3+1 = 7.

A flowers = 3, B stars = 2, C circles = 1, D hexagons = 6.

The numbers in the rectangles represent the total of each column with the symbol values added together.

7. Check for types of shape. It is unlikely that there would be a fish among the birds, a hat among the shoes or a triangle among pentagons. What is the odd one out here? (It is nothing to do with the direction of the vehicles.)

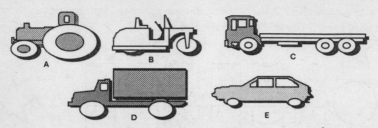

The odd one out is E. It is the only non-commercial vehicle in the selection.

8. Check for if-then sequence or reversal. If A = x includes y, and B = y includes x, and C = x includes x, it is logical that the next in the series should be D = y includes y. What should replace the question mark in this series?

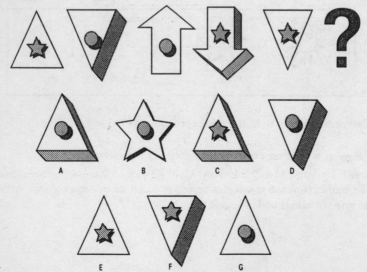

The next in sequence is A. Where 2 is 1 flipped upside down with a three-dimensional shape added, the sequence is s/1, c/2, c/1, s/2, s/1, c/2 = A.

9. Finally, check all the alternatives. In the following illustration, the footballers can move like chess knights in L-shaped moves of two horizontal and one vertical square or vice versa. They can land on any colour. There are no diagonal moves. They cannot land on any square with a footballer. What is the minimum number of moves that each will take to reach the square with the ball?

1._____ moves   2._____ moves

3._____ moves   4._____ moves

5._____ moves   6._____ moves

Man 1:3 moves, Man 2:5 moves, Man 3:2 moves, Man 4:2 moves, Man 5:4 moves, Man 6:2 moves

10. Focus on the detail. Two things can be broadly similar, yet different in detail, as in the classic test of observation where you have to spot differences:

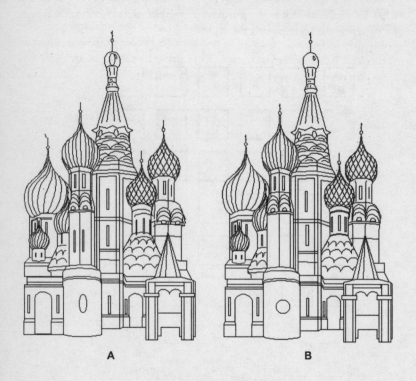

A   B

These observation type problems are often included in aptitude tests for jobs that require a good eye for detail, such as the electronics industry. But if you didn't spot most of the changes it could simply be that you require a new pair of spectacles.

You should now have a broad grasp of the concepts behind visual-spatial tests. The following problems combine various aspects of these concepts. See if you can do them. Bear in mind that it takes at least three times as long to learn a concept as it does to read about it. There is no time limitation on these tests because the object is to get them done, no matter how long it takes, in order to learn the principles involved. If you cheat by turning to the answers before putting in your best efforts, it is like trying to learn how to drive by sitting in an armchair being told how to drive. It won't work.

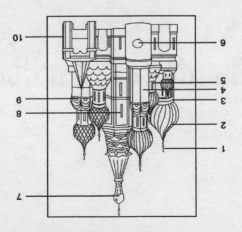

Visual–Spatial Practice Test 1

1. Which of the numbered shapes – A, B, C, D, E or F – should continue the sequence?

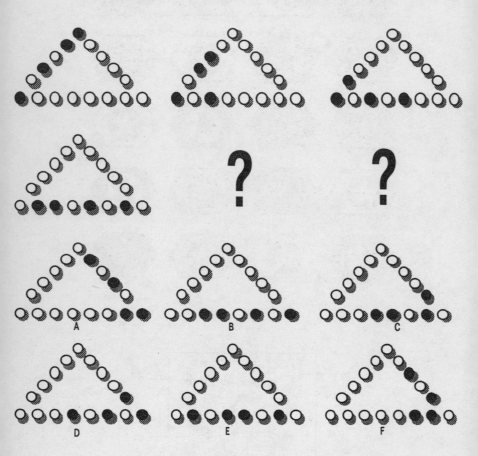

2. Which row breaks the sequence?

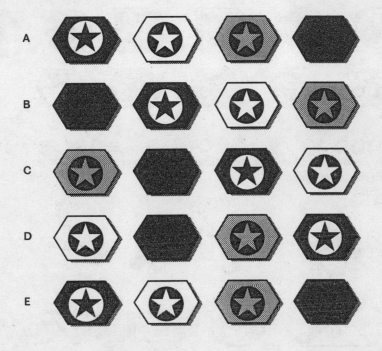

3. What comes next, A, B, C, D or E?

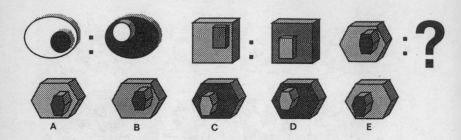

4. In each of the following groups, circle the object that does not go with the other three.

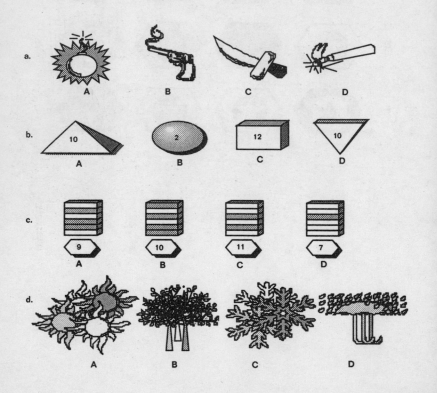

5. How many white donkeys are there in this herd?

6. Which of the numbered shapes should continue the sequence?

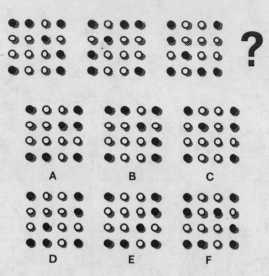

7. Which tile comes next?

A

B

C

D

E

F

8. What replaces the blanks?

Example:

▸	✓	▸
◂	▸	▸
3	5	4

▸	✓	◂
✓	✓	◂
5	6	2

▸	◂	✓
4	4	1
6	5	4

❉	❊	❊
❊	❊	❊
4	5	6

❉	❊	❉
❉	❊	❉
3	2	4

❊	❊	❉
5	3	3

2	1	2

A

3	1	1

B

2	2	2

C

2	2	1

D

1	1	2

E

1	3	3

F

9. Which shape comes next in each sequence?

10. There is something wrong with the sequence of tiles in the group of nine. Find the error and identify the tile – A, B, C, D, E or F – that should replace it.

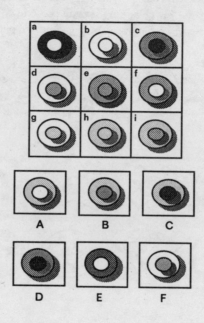

SCORING

If you solved more than three of these you are better than average at visual-spatial tests. If you scored less, don't feel bad. You may still be better than average at these problems, because this book is aimed at readers who are above average. If you solved most of them, you have a very high visual-spatial IQ. The next set will provide you with further challenges, and you can concentrate on developing speed.

Visual–Spatial Practice Test 2

1. Draw a continuous line through the maze to show the shortest route to the tree. If you draw more than one line, you get no marks.

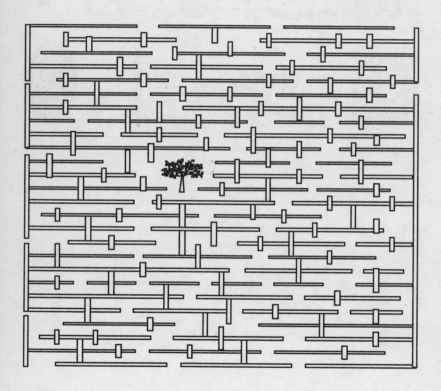

2. Which shape – A, B, C or D – comes next?

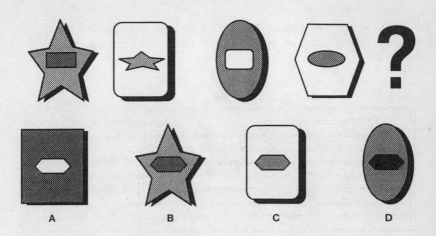

A   B   C   D

3. Using the first letter of the name of the objects, find a route from the top to the bottom of the honeycomb that provides another name for readers of this book.

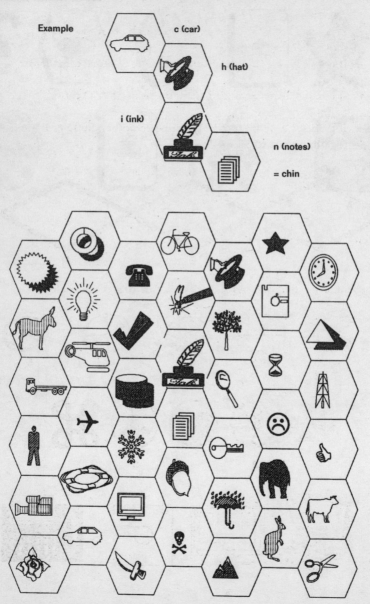

4. The points marked with letters on this wire frame are swivel points.

   a. If point A is pushed in the direction of E, does C move in the direction of B or F?
   b. If points G & H are moved towards each other, do B & E move together or apart?
   c. If points B & E are pulled apart, do G & H move together or apart?
   d. If points C & F are pulled apart, do points A & D move together or apart?
   e. If points B & E are moved towards each other, do D & F move together or apart?

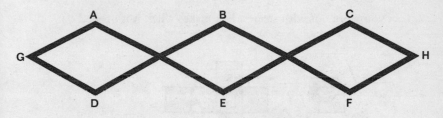

5. Identify the odd one out in each group in 10 seconds each.

6. Which shape – A, B, C, D or E – comes next?

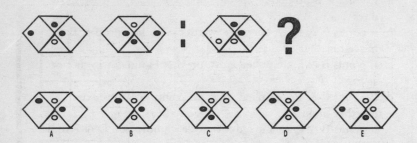

7. Can you work out what shape a box makes when it is opened out?

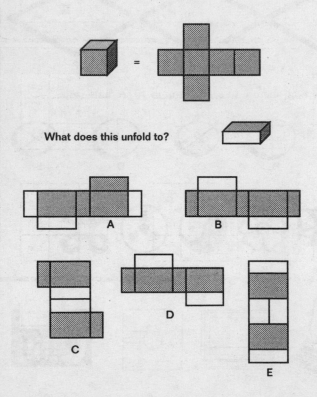

What does this unfold to?

8. Which tile comes next – A, B, C, D, E or F?

9. Which shape — A, B, C, D or E — is the odd one out?

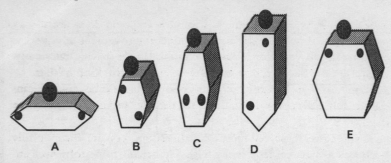

10. These blocks are designed to confuse. Which group — A, B, C, D, E or F — should replace the question mark? (Balls can change position within blocks, but cannot move to blocks of a different colour.)

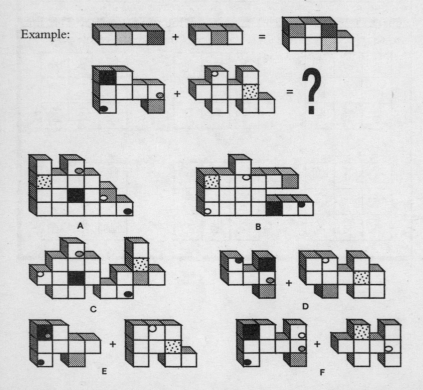

SCORING

You should have a fair idea by now of how well you do at visual-spatial tests and you should have noticed a distinct improvement in your performance. If you scored over five in this last set (having previously completed the first set), you are above average at this kind of tests. Although they are designed so that, given sufficient time, anyone can do them, many people do not have the patience required to complete them.

If you correctly solved most of the questions, you are exceptionally good at visual-spatial tests, and you should be able to perform well at any culture-fair or similar test. If you got fewer than three correct, do not despair. Although you may not have a natural aptitude for visual-spatial tests, you will improve with practice. Try going back to the beginning of this chapter and working your way through it again. It often happens that when we first look at a problem the solution evades us, but when we return to it with fresh eyes, we find that our subconscious has been working on it and the solution comes. This, it is worth repeating, is the best reason to read through the whole paper before starting work on any test.

Principles of Logic

• •

Logic enables us to discriminate between truth and lies and to make the best possible decisions in any given set of circumstances, basing our decisions only on things that are relevant. With logic, we don't say what we feel, we say what we know. Take the following example:

An intelligent young girl with only one arm has three balls – one red; one green; one blue. She can discriminate all other colours but is colour–blind to red. She does not know the colour of the red ball.

Which of the following can she say with certainty? (Each statement is to be considered in isolation.)

a. I have a red ball.
b. Looking through this lens, which I know to be red, I can tell that this ball is red, because it is the only ball that changes colour.
c. Looking through this lens, which I know to be red, I can tell this ball is red, because it is the only ball that does not change colour.
d. I have a green ball, a blue ball and another ball.
e. I can see this ball best in the dark, so this ball must be red.
f. Since I can see the colour of the blue ball and the green ball, this other ball must be red.
g. I have a blue ball.
h. I have a ball that is invisible to me.
i. I have a ball of a colour which may or may not be red.
j. I have a ball of a colour which I cannot determine.

The girls's intelligence and one-armedness are red herrings and have no effect on the answers. Only b, c, d, e, g, i and j can be said with certainty. a. she doesn't know. b. is wrong. A red lens won't change a red colour. c. is correct. d. is correct, as we have already been told in the phrasing of the original statement. e. is wrong. In total darkness none of the balls will be seen. In less than total darkness the colour of the ambient light will determine which ball can best be seen. f. can't be said with certainty. We have not been told that she knows she has a red ball. g. is correct. h. is a logical error. The ball is visible, it is the colour that cannot be determined. i. is correct. j is correct.

In the above example, as in most questions of logic, only the relevant information given in the original problem can be used to determine the truth or falsehood of any statement. If you assume what you don't know, you can go wrong. This principle of non-assumption can be used to increase our IQ score and improve the quality of our judgement in many aspects of everyday life. When you are learning:

- Don't assume that you know what a new word means until you have looked it up. If there is the slightest chance that you have misspelled or misunderstood a word, look it up.

- Don't assume that you have mastered a subject after doing a single example. Revision is essential.

When you are doing IQ tests:

- Don't assume that similar questions will have similar instructions. Read all instructions carefully.

- Don't assume that you automatically get things right first time. Many problems in life and in IQ tests involve discrimination between several possible options. There may be a better choice.

- Don't assume that the most difficult questions in a set will be the later ones. Glance through them all before you start. Do those you can do most easily first.

Similarly, in life:

- Don't assume that you know anything about a person from his or her appearance, race, colour, or religion. Get to know the real person before making up your mind.

- Don't assume that your boss knows how good you are. Be conspicuously better than others.

- Don't assume that anything will change if you do nothing to change things.

- Don't assume that, if you have failed in the past, you'll fail in the future.

- Don't assume that you know what you don't know.

Simple logic can be used both to eliminate impossible options, and to draw unequivocal conclusions. For example, if black = 4 and white = 6, then black + white = 10. However, if we do not know the value of white, we cannot possibly know the result of black + white. What we will know is that unless white is a negative number, the result of black + white will be equal to or greater than 4.

Aristotle invented the use of mathematical logic in the form of the syllogism, which is the logical deduction of one conclusion made from two facts.

Fact: All mammals are warm blooded. Fact: Elephants are warm blooded. Conclusion: Elephants are mammals.

Although this may seem rather obvious, it is the beginning of logical reasoning, and the process can be used to reach more complex conclusions in a step-by-step approach. For example, if you are on a roof, and it is a high pitched roof, and you are unable to balance, and you are not a rubber ball, and you are unable to fly, and you are not part of the roof, then you may be in danger unless you are tied on or are in a place with no gravity, or are already dead. There is no limit to the number of factors that can be taken into account, and your short-term memory may be tested as much as your ability to reach logical conclusions. In fact, we all use syllogism to a certain extent when making judgements about people, events, possibilities and decisions.

Beware of faulty logic leading you to wrong conclusions. For example, the statement 'If you are being followed then someone will be behind you,' is logical, but the conclusion, 'There is someone behind me, therefore I am being followed,' is clearly faulty. The person behind you could simply be another innocent pedestrian.

Again: 'All lions have four legs and a tail,' is a fairly accurate generalization, but to say: 'This animal has four legs and a tail, therefore this animal is a lion,' is an obvious error of reasoning.

This logic can be illustrated in a Venn diagram:

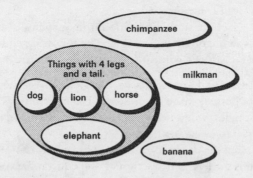

It can be seen in the diagram that although lions do belong to the set of 'things that have four legs and a tail', lions have their own distinct subset, and other animals that have a place in the set of 'things with four legs and a tail' are not to be considered part of the subset 'lions', just as the banana, chimpanzee, and milkman cannot claim a place in the set of 'things with four legs and a tail'.

Venn diagrams can be used to test the logic of many propositions, and they have the advantage of being quick and easy to produce. You can sketch one in a margin in a few seconds.

Most logic problems involve selecting the correct option from a number of possible choices, with varying levels of discrimination between the options. For example, after having a fatal heart attack during an IQ test, you arrive at the gates of heaven and St Peter decides to test your ability to discriminate truth before he will let you enter. He puts you into a room with six doors, and tells you that the least contradictory door is the one that will let you in. However, you know that he is lying and that the opposite of what he says is true. Which door lets you into heaven?

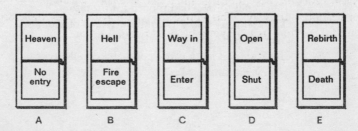

The answer is D (an 'open and shut case'). Now look back and decide which door you would enter if St Peter had been telling the truth. The answer is C (the least contradictory).

The ability to gain practical information from graphical representation is an important logical skill. The following illustration is the half-year sales chart of a company that supplies software, monitors and fax machines.

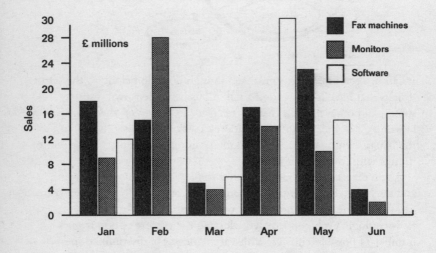

Study the chart and decide which of the following statements are certainly true (T), which are possible, but not necessarily true (P) and which are certainly false (F).

    a. February was the top month for fax machines.
    b. May was the top month for software.
    c. March was the worst month overall.
    d. June tends to be a bad month for monitors.
    e. The company sold £80 million worth of monitors over the half-year.
    f. If it had tried harder, the company could have achieved more in March.

The anwers are: a. F (it was May); b. F (it was April); c. T; d. P (the shown period may not be typical); e. F (it was less than £70 million); f. P (the low March sales could be the result of anything).

You should be aware that many tests deliberately use ridiculous postulations in order to distract your attention from the simple logic involved. The statements do not have to be sensible for the logic to work. For example:

a. If a dog is a bus, and has all the properties of a bus, could it bite you?
b. If a worm + a bird = a cat, and a cat is worth two worms, is a bird worth more than a worm?
c. Some credit cards are motorbikes and some pigs are motorbikes, therefore some pigs are credit cards.
d. Some brown is green, and some brown is white, but no green is white. All brown can fly, but no brown can sing. Some green can sing. Therefore some white can fly.

Although the propositions use absurd subjects, the answers may be logically deduced: a. No. A dog that has all the properties of a bus *is* a bus; b. No: if w + b = c, and c is worth 2 times w, then b = w; c. False: because some credit cards are motorbikes, and some pigs are motorbikes, does not necessarily mean that some credit cards will be pigs, as illustrated in the Venn diagram, in which the shaded area is the area of commonality;

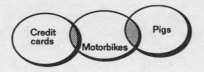

d. True: as can be seen from the Venn diagram below; the key statements are 'some brown is white' and 'all brown can fly'; The other statements are red herrings.

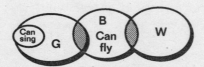

If you managed the previous examples without too much difficulty, you should have no major problems with the logical/reasoning side of IQ tests. You have, in fact, already completed many tests involving logic in the other chapters of this book. No problem can be solved without using logic to help you find the solution, and if you improve your logical/reasoning abilities, you will improve all areas likely to be tested in IQ problems.

Finally, beware of the logical error known as 'circular argument'. For example, *'I know my partner is faithful to me because she tells me so, and I know that what she tells me is true because she is she is faithful to me,'* is a classic circular argument. Whether your partner is or is not faithful, you would be naïve to be convinced by that argument. Again, *'I know the defendant is guilty because he is charged with the crime, and he is charged with the crime because he is guilty,'* is a circular argument that could scarcely be considered sufficient evidence to secure a conviction.

The following practice sessions will help to refine your logical/reasoning skill and will introduce some types of problems with which you may not yet be familiar.

Logical Deduction Practice Test 1

1. If 3 is 5 and 5 is 7, what is 3 x 5 x 2?

2. If Jack sits to the left of Mary, and Mary sits to the left of Lucy, and Lucy sits further right than Jack, who is in the middle?

3. With the colours ranked on a scale of 1 to 5, if green is worth five times the value of red, and pink is worth twice the value of yellow, give the colours – green, red, pink, yellow and blue – their values.

4. If cats are eaten by dogs, and fish eat dogs, and people are eaten by cats, what is at the top of the food chain?

5. In a children's home there are 12 girls called Elizabeth with red hair, nine girls called Linda with black hair, six boys called Julio with white hair, and two boys and two girls called Sandy with red hair, but no others unmentioned. Judge the truth (T) or falsehood (F) of the following statements, using the criterion that if a statement is not necessarily true, it is to be considered false:

   a. There are more than twice as many girls with red hair than boys with white hair.
   b. The girls called Elizabeth weigh more than the girls called Sandy.
   c. There are three times as many girls as boys in the home.
   d. The boys called Sandy are embarrassed by having the same name as the girls called Sandy.
   e. If three of the girls called Linda changed their names to Elizabeth, there would still be fewer than two times as many girls called Elizabeth than there were called Linda before the name change.
   f. If each girl was two sausages, and these sausages were divided between the two boys called Sandy, they would be able to have seven meals of three sausages each, and one meal of one sausage each.

6. Is the following statement true (T) or false (F)?

> Some dreams are pianos, and all pianos can walk. Also, some
> dreams are tables and all tables can eat. Therefore, some pianos
> can eat.

7. A black rubber ball and a white rubber ball are simultaneously
dropped on a no-atmosphere moon that has a gravity of one-third that
on earth. If the white ball weighs three times as much as the black ball,
indicate which of the following are true or false, using the Martian
conditioning factors that if something is necessarily false it is false, but if
it is not necessarily false it is true. (Clue: On earth, ignoring the effects
of atmospheric resistance, all objects fall at the same speed. In a vacuum,
a feather falls as fast as a lump of coal.)

   a. The white ball will land first.
   b. The white ball will drop, but the black ball will not fall.
   c. The white ball will not fall, and the black ball will rise up.
   d. Both balls will explode.
   e. Both balls will land at the same time.
   f. A thrown ball will travel further than it would if thrown
      with the same force on a similar moon with a higher
      gravity.

8. In a family of three children, Jon sometimes tells lies, Susanne always
says the exact opposite of the truth, and Ricardo tells the truth only on
Sundays. They all know the answer to an important question. Answer
the following:

   a. Who is the best person to ask for the answer on the day that
      is three days before the day that is two days after the day
      that is three days before Thursday?
   b. Who is the best person to ask for the answer on the day that
      is three days after the day that is two days before Friday?
   c. Who is the worst person to ask for the answer on the day
      that is four days before the day that is three days after the
      day that is a day before Wednesday?

9. The first day after planting a fast-growing waterlily it covers an area of 1 × 1 metre of a pond that measures 32m × 32 metres. It doubles in size every day until it entirely covers the pond.

    a. On which day will the entire pond be covered?
    b. On which day will half the pond be covered?
    c. On which day will the lily cover eight times the area that it covered on the first day?

10. Kati deals in antique watches, and she has two broken Swiss watches worth 120 credits each when working. If she manages to sell both watches when they have been repaired, she will get their full value, but it will cost her 60 credits each to have them repaired. However, if she allows the watchmaker to keep the parts from one of the watches, she can have the other one repaired free of charge. Name two things Kati needs to know to be able to make the best profit-oriented decision?

SCORING

Points score × 100 ÷ 24 = Percentage score_____

This set will have given you a good idea of how much work you have to do to improve your logical/reasoning abilities. If you had great difficulty getting through the set you have a lot of work to do. If you found the tests easy, you will find greater challenges ahead. A score of around 30 per cent on this test is about average. With a score of over 70 per cent you will outperform almost every rival on the logical sections of IQ tests, depending, of course, on how long you allowed yourself to complete the tests. The faster you did them, the more your score means, but since the point of the practice sessions is to learn the concepts, it is possible that the faster you did the tests, the less you learned.

Logical Deduction Practice Test 2

1. There are two routes to the diamond on this map. You may enter the arrow grid only through an arrow that is pointing in the direction of your travel. For example, if you enter through a five arrow, you travel in the direction that the arrow is pointing in for five moves. Circle the entrance arrow, and plot the route to the diamond.

2. Decode the following hieroglyphics to find a valuable message left to us by Jeremias Gotthelf.

Key: a is to ♋ as z is to ⌘

3. Lillie has two pairs of red shoes, but none that are blue. She has no other two pairs the same colour as each other. Mary has one pair of shoes the same colour as Lillie's matching pairs, and a white pair. Daniel has three pairs of black shoes and a favourite pair that are the same colour as the only pair of Mary's shoes that are not the same colour as Lillie's two matching pairs. Lillie has a pair the same colour as Daniel's favourite pair. Mary, Lillie and Daniel have no other pairs of shoes.

Which of the following statements are true (T), and which are false, using the logic that only that which can be said with certainty is true, and that which cannot be said with certainty is false?

   a. Lillie has no white shoes.
   b. Daniel has no red shoes.
   c. Daniel has a pair of white shoes.
   d. Lillie needs more shoes.
   e. Mary has one pair of shoes the same colour as a pair of Daniel's.
   f. Mary has two pairs of shoes that are not the same colour as any of Daniel's or Lillie's shoes.
   g. Mary has one pair of red shoes.
   h. Daniel has four pairs of shoes, none of which is the same colour as the pair of Mary's shoes that are the same colour as Lillie's matching two pairs.

4. Kevin has three unopened eggs, but he suspects one of them to be bad. Using the same logic as above, which of the following statements can he say for certain?

   a. If I open two of these, and neither of them is rotten, I will know that the third egg is rotten.
   b. I can safely eat two of these eggs.
   c. Two of these eggs are not rotten.
   d. One of these eggs is rotten.
   e. One of these eggs may be rotten.
   f. All of these eggs may be rotten.
   g. None of these eggs may be rotten.
   h. If I eat one of these eggs and I am sick, I will know that was the rotten one.
   i. Rotten eggs float. If one of these eggs floats, I will know it is rotten.

5. Mary has been married three times. Once to Michael, once to Andrew and once to Sandy, but not in that order. She had two children to each husband: Sheila and Lorraine to Andrew; Fred and Anne to Sandy; and Patrick and Sean to Michael.

   a. If Patrick and Sean are older than Sheila and Lorraine, and Fred and Anne are older than Sheila and Lorraine, and Patrick and Sean are younger than Fred and Anne, which husband did Mary marry first, which second and which third?

   b. If Sean is the combined ages of Fred & Anne, and Fred is three times the age of Anne, and Sheila is three times the age of Sean, and two years older than Lorraine who is 10, what are the ages of Sheila, Fred, Anne, Lorraine and Sean?

6. If a super-grow formula makes a prize honeysuckle double in size every day, until at the end of 40 days it completely covers the wall against which it is growing, how long would it take:

   a. Two identical plants with the same growing capacity to cover the same wall?

   b. Four identical plants with the same growing capacity to cover the same wall?

7. Using the scales below, determine the values of the minimum number of weights that a shopkeeper needs to weigh any items between 1 and 15 units, to the nearest unit?

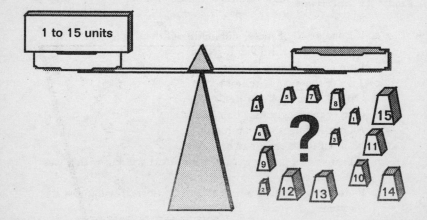

8. Almost 2500 years ago, in his various paradoxes such as the Flying
Arrow, the Stadium, the Moving Rows and Achilles and the Tortoise,
Zeno of Elea put forward the proposition, based on spatial division, that
motion is impossible. His puzzles continue to baffle many people even
now. See if you can solve the Flying Arrow paradox.

> If an arrow is fired from a bow, it must travel half the distance
> to the target, then half the remaining distance, then again half
> the remaining distance and so on, the divisions continually
> becoming smaller and smaller towards infinity. How is it
> possible for the arrow to cover an infinite number of divisions
> of distance in a finite time?

9. In a dentist's queue the patients will be taken from left to right (from
an observer's point of view). Lana sits to the right of Kevin. Jack sits
two to the left of Lana. Two people separate Lana and Mark. Consider
each of the following problems independently.

   a. Who will be the first, second, third and last to be taken?
   b. If Jack and Lana swap places, what will be the new left to right
      order?
   c. If Jack and Lana swap places and the first in the queue now
      swaps places with the last in the queue, what will be the new
      left-to-right order?

10. Suggest a method by which the centre of balance (centre of gravity)
of this following plywood board may be easily found.

SCORING

Points score $\times 100 \div 54$ = Percentage score_____ .

This set was a shade more difficult than the previous set, so if you managed about the same percentage score in this set, you have improved your logical and reasoning abilities.

If you scored around 30 per cent on this test you are probably about average for readers of this book, but somewhat above the average of the general population as a whole.

With a score of around 50 per cent you will perform well on most promotion or college entrance tests. With a score of over 70 per cent you are probably in the top 2 per cent of the population, operating at the same level as top doctors, scientists and engineers. Whatever your score, long-term improvement will come only by stretching your abilities to and beyond their limits.

Logical Deduction Practice Test 3

1. Complete the following analogies.

a. master is to nbtufs as slave is to _____.

b. 1221288 is to madness as genius is to _____.

2. James has a pack of cards from which some are missing. Originally there were 52 cards in the pack. If the pack is dealt equally among five people, two cards are left over. If the pack is dealt equally among four people, three cards are left over. If it is dealt equally among six people, five cards are left over. How many cards are missing from the pack?

3. What is the value of the individual shapes in the following puzzle?

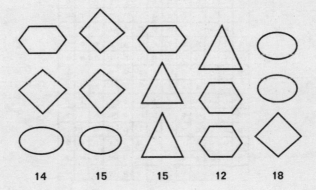

| 14 | 15 | 15 | 12 | 18 |

4. In the following word grid, find the single words that mean the same as the following. Words will be found up, down, backwards, forwards and diagonally. Not all the clues are straightforward. For example, tree-climbers gives the solution coons, as shown in the shaded squares.

1. hideaway; 2. smash; 3. pain; 4. hurry; 5. hello; 6. interior; 7. instruct; 8. strike; 9. stain; 10. exposed; 11. stumbles; 12. sow; 13. effortlessly; 14. flexible; 15. poison; 16. lonesome; 17. misplaced; 18. lawn game' 19. completely; 20. brave; 21. concluder; 22. lazy; 23. jog; 24. goddess; 25. falsehood; 26. female; 27. runner; 28. stripe; 29. flower bush; 30. footwear; 31. garden implement; 32. drug; 33. type; 34. rook-type bird; 35. large plants; 36. man; 37. turn; 38. knock; 39. pudding; 40. god of love; 41. particle; 42. carpet; 43. joint; 44. wrong doing; 45. vegetable; 46. cake; 47. stair; 48. boys; 49. grieve; 50. seats; 51. mind-science; 52. environmental biology; 53. city; 54. tree climbers; 56. present

y	l	l	a	t	o	t	s	r	i	a	h	c
g	a	a	s	h	e	h	o	e	s	o	r	a
o	y	o	m	n	o	u	p	p	i	a	a	r
l	l	i	n	e	t	r	i	p	s	w	c	r
o	i	i	s	s	n	g	u	h	i	o	e	o
h	s	i	i	a	u	t	m	u	n	h	r	t
c	a	d	a	r	i	n	g	r	u	s	h	i
y	e	l	a	s	t	i	c	t	r	a	i	n
s	s	e	o	e	s	n	o	s	p	e	t	s
p	w	b	u	n	n	k	i	n	r	w	r	i
i	o	n	o	i	e	r	e	d	i	c	e	d
e	r	o	s	c	i	o	a	n	n	p	e	e
e	c	o	l	o	g	y	e	p	t	n	s	r

5. Three years ago Jake's grandson was a tenth of the age that Jake is now; Jake's son was a half of the age that Jake is now, and his granddaughter was a third of the age of his son. Newton, his granddaughter's dog, was half of her age, and her cat Galileo, who is now six, was two years younger than the dog. What age are Jake, his son, his grandson, his granddaughter, Newton and Galileo now?

6. If the bus is late, Juan will miss his meeting. If the bus is not late, Juan will miss the bus. Is it possible for Juan to keep his meeting?

7. Reorganize the following words into four logical groups:

shrivelling	reduction	amplify	contract
enlarge	diminish	expansion	growth
constriction	develop	increment	elision
shrink	swelling	reduce	expand

8. In a class of eight children, John has black hair and white teeth; Margot has black hair and red teeth; and Carlos has red hair and black teeth. Aggy and Missy both have teeth the same colour as Carlos's hair, and hair the same colour as John; and Margareeta and Curly have hair the same colour as Carlos's teeth, and teeth the same colour as John. Jean has hair the same colour as Margareeta's hair, and Jean's teeth are the same colour as John's hair.

State which of the following are certainly true (T), false (F) or possible (P).

a. Some of the group have red hair and red teeth.
b. Curly has white hair and black teeth.
c. Aggy has red teeth and black hair.
d. Carlos and John come from different families.
e. Jean has red hair and white teeth.
f. Missy, Aggy and Curly belong to the same sub-group, in terms of teeth and hair
g. Jean, Carlos and Margareeta belong to the same sub-group in terms of teeth and hair.
h. All of those in the sub-group with red hair have black teeth.
i. All of those with black hair have white teeth.
j. Those with black teeth need to brush their teeth more.

9. While Jane was waiting for a train she timed one that passed her travelling at 60 kilometres per hour. It took exactly four seconds to pass her. What was the length of the train?

10. In 15 years the combined ages of two married couples will be 390.

a. What are their combined ages now?
b. What will their combined ages be in 12 years?
c. What will be the combined ages of the survivors in 20 years if one of the men dies at the age of 80, in five years time?

SCORING

Points score × 2 = Percentage score_____.

This set contained more applied logic than the previous set, so if you managed about the same percentage score, your logical and reasoning ability has a practical side that should be very useful to you. If you increased your percentage score substantially, you have almost certainly improved.

Your score on this test will depend a lot on the time that you gave yourself to do it. The longer you spent, the less your score will mean in terms of current IQ score. However, if you spent a long time completing the tests and persisted through difficulty to achieve the (mostly) correct answers, you have the qualities necessary to achieve success in any venture. Persistence wins through every time.

General Knowledge

• •

No matter how quick-witted we are, if we don't know much about the world in which we live people will not respect our intelligence. A lack of knowledge can even make us the laughing-stock among acquaintances: 'What! You've never heard of John Steinbeck? What planet have you been living on?' This can be irritating, especially when it comes from someone with a one-track mind, but they may have a point. Even the most intelligent people can get into the habit of ignoring opportunities to find things out. We let things go over our heads without investigating them. That's inertia, a physical law that affects people just as much as it affects inanimate objects.

Just as a deadline, whether adopted or imposed, forces us to conquer our procrastination, completing a set task can help to overcome our investigative inertia. So here's a task: complete the following general knowledge quiz. There are 10 sets of 10 questions, with the answers at the end. When you mark each set, look up the details of the questions you got wrong. Information acquired by investigation is always retained better than that which you are simply told. Active learning is better than passive learning.

If you find some of the subjects trivial, irrelevant or uninteresting, bear in mind that as we grow in knowledge, we also grow in wisdom. If that were not so, we would never grow in character.

General Knowledge Questions

Keep a note of your scores.

SET 1

1. The blue peter flag means:
   a. Royalty on board
   b. I am about to sail
   c. I am carrying mail

2. The Duke of Edinburgh's father was:
   a. King Olav
   b. King Gustav
   c. Prince Andrew

3. Plato got his name because:
   a. He had broad shoulders
   b. He was into platonic relationships
   c. He was named after the planet Pluto

4. When a person is smoking, the rate of his or her heartbeat:
   a. Increases
   b. Decreases
   c. Doesn't change

5. Hang-gliding started in:
   a. 1930s
   b. 1890s
   c. 1960s

6. Penicillin was discovered by:
   a. Alexander Fleming
   b. Edward Jenner
   c. Marie Curie

7. *War and Peace* was written by:
   a. Leo Tolstoy
   b. J.R.R. Tolkien
   c. John Lennon

8. Yeast is:
   a. A single-cell fungus
   b. A single-cell animal
   c. A single-cell plant

9. The first west Europeans to settle in America were:
   a. French
   b. Spanish
   c. British

10. Edward de Bono invented:
    a. Mind mapping
    b. Bonio, the pet food
    c. Lateral thinking

SET 2

1. The national emblem of Germany is:
   a. The iron cross
   b. The eagle
   c. The torch

2. Anthony Burgess was:
   a. A Soviet spy
   b. A novelist
   c. A politician

3. The largest ocean in the world is the:
   a. Arctic
   b. Atlantic
   c. Pacific

4. Hanoi is in:
   a. Vietnam
   b. Cambodia
   c. China

5. Britain's first prime minister was:
   a. Sir Robert Walpole
   b. William Pitt
   c. Sir Robert Peel

6. The gramophone was invented by:
   a. Graham A. Fpoene
   b. King George IV
   c. Thomas Edison

7. The *Mona Lisa* was painted by:
   a. Michelangelo
   b. Raphael
   c. Leonardo da Vinci

8. Kinematics is the study of:
   a. The cinema
   b. Moving systems
   c. Heat energy

9. The earth orbits the sun in:
   a. 24 hours
   b. 28 days
   c. 365 days

10. The normal number of chromosomes for a human is:
    a. 46
    b. 26
    c. 42

SET 3

1. Modern human beings are known as:
   a. *Homo sapiens*
   b. *Homo habilis*
   c. *Homo erectus*

2. Dick Whittington was a famous:
   a. Prime minister
   b. Lord mayor
   c. Highway robber

3. Jet engines run on:
   a. Kerosene
   b. High-octane petrol
   c. Liquid oxygen

4. Voltaire was:
   a. A writer
   b. An inventor
   c. An electrical engineer

5. Magnesium sulphate is:
   a. Toothpaste
   b. Milk of Magnesia
   c. Plaster of Paris

6. The Roman letter used to signify 50 is:
   a. L
   b. VC
   c. XXXXX

7. In a metre there are:
   a. 1000 centimetres
   b. 1000 micrometres
   c. 1000 millimetres

8. Before he became President of the United States, Richard Nixon was:
   a. A lawyer
   b. A used-car salesman
   c. A psychiatrist

9. Guinea pigs are related to:
   a. Mice
   b. Pigs
   c. Deer

10. Marco Polo:
    a. Invented Polo Mints
    b. Was a famous traveller
    c. Invented the game of polo

SET 4

1. The 365-day calendar was first used around:
   a. 4500 years ago
   b. 2500 years ago
   c. 250 years ago

2. Pantophobia is the fear of:
   a. Underpants
   b. Oxygen deficiency
   c. Everything

3. *Paradise Lost* was written by:
   a. Neil Diamond
   b. John Milton
   c. Homer

4. Australia was discovered by:
   a. Captain James Cook
   b. Willem Jansz
   c. John Cabot

5. An autocrat is:
   a. Wealthy
   b. Domineering
   c. Aristocratic

6. Nuclear power stations work by:
   a. Fusion
   b. Fission
   c. Controlled explosion

7. The speed of light is:
   a. 186,000 miles per second
   b. 186,000 miles per minute
   c. 186,000 miles per hour

8. Bolivia is near:
   a. Germany
   b. Czechoslovakia
   c. Brazil

9. Fortissimo means:
   a. Very loud
   b. Very quiet
   c. Use forethought

10. The SALT-2 arms limitation treaty was signed in:
    a. Geneva
    b. Vienna
    c. Rome

Set 5

1. The best-selling book of all time is:
   a. Quotations from the works of Mao Zedong
   b. The Bible
   c. The Koran

2. Agricola is or was:
   a. A soft drink
   b. A Roman governor of Britain
   c. An agricultural-waste coal substitute

3. In Xanadu did Kubla Khan:
   a. Build caverns measureless to man
   b. Start the War of the Roses
   c. A stately pleasure dome decree

4. Hippocrates was:
   a. An outrageous hypocrite
   b. The originator of the 'eureka' principle
   c. A physician

5. The most widely occurring metal in the earth's crust is:
   a. Tin
   b. Iron
   c. Aluminium

6. Billy the Kid's real name was:
   a. William H. Bonney
   b. William Frederick Cody
   c. William Wallace

7. The motto of the modern Olympic movement is:
   a. Who dares wins
   b. Beware Greeks bearing gifts
   c. Faster, higher, stronger

8. The word 'hamster' means in German:
   a. Tastes like ham
   b. Storer
   c. Big bottom

9. *The Adventures of Tom Sawyer* was written by:
   a. Charles Dickens
   b. Charlotte Brontë
   c. Mark Twain

10. Sodium chloride is:
    a. Caustic soda
    b. Common salt
    c. Bleach

SET 6

1. Valhalla is:
   a. An opera hall in Venice
   b. The Norse heaven for warrior heroes
   c. The north wind

2. Jonathan Swift wrote:
   a. *Gulliver's Travels*
   b. The American Constitution
   c. *Pickwick Papers*

3. *For Whom the Bell Tolls* was written by:
   a. Gabriel García Márquez
   b. Kingsley Amis
   c. Ernest Hemingway

4. Coal is a form of:
   a. Silicon
   b. Carbon
   c. Nitrogen

5. The first gun was invented in:
   a. 245BC
   c. 945AD
   b. 1545AD

6. Astronomers estimate the total lifespan of our sun to be:
   a. 10 billion years
   b. 10 million years
   c. 1 million years

7. Humpback whales are:
   a. Fish
   b. Mammals
   c. Amphibious reptiles

8. Telepathy is:
   a. The ability to communicate mind to mind
   b. The psychic ability to move objects
   c. The ability to see the future

9. Oberon was:
   a. The king of the fairies
   b. The Greek god of mediocre writing
   c. The name of the first Atom bomb

10. *Of Mice and Men* was written by:
    a. Mickey Spillane
    b. Laurence Sterne
    c. John Steinbeck

SET 7

1. Referring to sleep, the initials REM mean:
   a. Really exhausted mode
   b. Relaxed erotic micro movements
   c. Rapid eye movement

2. Mikhail Gorbachev was awarded:
   a. The Pulitzer Prize
   b. The Nobel Peace Prize
   c. A British Knighthood

3. A spider is:
   a. An insect
   b. An animal
   c. An anaconda

4. The first person to introduce tobacco to Britain was:
   a. Sir Walter Raleigh
   b. Sir Francis Drake
   c. Christopher Columbus

5. The Maori people live in:
   a. Polynesia
   b. New Zealand
   c. Central Africa

6. Oliver Cromwell lived:
   a. 1399 – 1458
   b. 1499 – 1558
   c. 1599 – 1658

7. Alfred Nobel was:
   a. The inventor of dynamite
   b. The King of Sweden
   c. King Alfred The Great

8. The country known as the 'Land of the Midnight Sun' is:
   a. Norway
   b. Japan
   c. Australia

9. The greenhouse effect causes:
   a. Carbon dioxide
   b. Global warming
   c. Global cooling

10. At Carthage the Romans:
    a. Held the first Olympic Games
    b. Destroyed the city
    c. Crucified Christ

SET 8

1. *Poor Richard's Almanac* was written by:
   a. Benjamin Franklin
   b. Francis Bacon
   c. Richard the Lionheart

2. Who said: 'All is for the best in the best of all possible worlds'
   a. Dr Pangloss
   b. Christ
   c. Margaret Thatcher

3. Mark Twain's real name was:
   a. Charles Dickens
   b. Samuel Langhorne Clemens
   c. Marcus Twickenham

4. The Great Fire of London was in:
   a. 1326
   b. 1666
   c. 1816

5. Ailurophobia is:
   a. The fear of getting ill
   b. The fear of young girls
   c. The fear of cats

6. Friedrich Neitzsche was:
   a. A Nazi leader
   b. A philosopher
   c. A religious leader

7. The steam engine was invented by:
   a. James Watt
   b. James Clerk Maxwell
   c. Thomas Newcome

8. The capital of Switzerland is:
   a. Stockholm
   b. Geneva
   c. Berne

9. Into the sun you could fit approximately:
   a. 100 earths
   b. 10,000 earths
   c. 1,000,000 earths

10. Charles Darwin worked out:
   a. The theory of relativity
   b. The theory of evolution
   c. The street plan of Darwin, Australia

SET 9

1. John Wilkes Booth was the person who:
   a. Killed President Lincoln
   b. Invented the telephone
   c. Invented the razor-blade

2. *Leaves of Grass* was written by:
   a. Robert Burns
   b. Bob Dylan
   c. Walt Whitman

3. Brazil is:
   a. An island
   b. A group of islands
   c. In South America

4. Mahatma Gandhi was assassinated in:
   a. 1928
   b. 1948
   c. 1968

5. The third planet from the sun is:
   a. Mars
   b. Earth
   c. Venus

6. *The Three Musketeers* was written by:
   a. Alexandre Dumas
   b. Joseph Conrad
   c. François Marie Arouet de Voltaire

7. The Japanese attacked Pearl Harbor in:
   a. December 1939
   b. December 1941
   c. December 1943

8. Ascorbic acid is:
   a. Caustic soda
   b. Baking powder
   c. Vitamin C

9. *One Day in the Life of Ivan Denisovich* was written by:
   a. Boris Pasternak
   b. Alexander Solzhenitsyn
   c. Ernest Hemingway

10. Iran was formerly called:
    a. Persia
    b. Iraq
    c. Kuwait

SET 10

1. D–Day was the day of:
   a. The Allied invasion of Europe
   b. The bombing of Hiroshima
   c. The British evacuation at Dunkirk

2. Who said: 'Being a President is like riding a tiger. A man has to keep on riding, or be swallowed'
   a. Harry S. Truman
   b. Richard M. Nixon
   c. John F. Kennedy

3. The cochlea is in:
   a. The genitalia
   b. The ear
   c. The brain

4. Ho Chi Minh was:
   a. Vietnamese
   b. Chinese
   c. Korean

5. Magna Carta was signed in:
   a. 1215
   b. 1415
   c. 1615

6. Who said: 'Give me a fixed point outside the earth to stand on, and I will move it'
   a. Albert Einstein
   b. Isaac Newton
   c. Archimedes

7. Napoleon Bonaparte was born in:
   a. 1669
   b. 1769
   c. 1869

8. *The Lord of the Flies* was written by:
   a. William Golding
   b. William Goldman
   c. Paul Goodman

9. Concentration camps were invented by:
   a. The Japanese
   b. The British
   c. The Germans

10. The initials ESP stand for:
    a. Educationally superior person
    b. European special police
    c. Extra-sensory perception

SCORING

Scores: Set 1_____
                Set 2_____
                Set 3_____
                Set 4_____
                Set 5_____
                Set 6_____
                Set 7_____
                Set 8_____
                Set 9_____
                Set 10_____
        Total Score_____

Score: 100 – 80 Excellent
79 – 60 Very good
59 – 40 Above average
39 – 20 Average
19 – 1 Below average

Whatever your score, the purpose of this quiz was to expose weaknesses in your general knowledge so that you can work to eliminate areas of weakness. Every subject is worth knowing and versatility is one of the keys to genius. If we are to cultivate the ability to think in ways that are unique and special, we need to assimilate as much information as we can about as many subjects as possible. Once we have the information, we can begin to look for links and use our new knowledge in a thousand different ways. Knowledge is never wasted; it is always useful.

IQ Test 2

Complete this test to check the improvement in your IQ after working your way through this book. The same rules apply as for the IQ Test 1 (see page 8).

1. Insert the connecting words, choosing from the list. For example, canary, <u>bird</u>, wren.

a. case, _____, bag
b. lizard, _____, snake
c. Bible, _____, Koran
d. gun, _____, knife
e. hammer, _____, saw
f. man, _____, woman
g. van, _____, car
h. boar, _____, hog
i. yacht, _____, liner
j. finger, _____, toe
k. beret, _____, trilby
l. sock, _____, shoe
m. red, _____, blue
n. much, _____, little
o. breed, _____, order

weapon, taste, foot, adder, war, battle, wood, colour, read, book, lies, lorry, child, reptile, category, boot, point, ferry, luggage, ship, animal, green, footwear, mate, head, how, value, pig, tree, hat, ruler, ink, person, shoot, bomb, briefcase, berry, vehicle, appendage, tool, cut, quantity

2. In each set of tiles (a, b and c), there are letters without numbers. Insert the missing numbers.

a.

a 2	c 4	e	g 4	i 16	k
b 2	d 3	f 9	h	j 5	l 25

b.

a	c 3	e 8	g 21	i 55	k
b 2	d	f 13	h	j 89	l 233

c.

a 15	c 14	e 2	g 13	i	k
b1	d14	f 12	h 3	j	l

3. Which shapes – A, B, C, D, E or F – should come next?

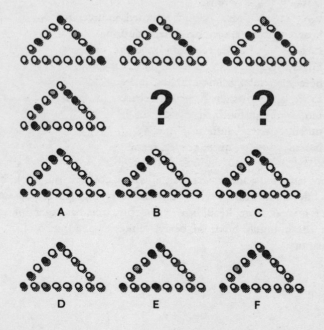

4. All black is good, and all yellow is bad. Some yellow is red. Some black is white, but no yellow is white. State whether the following are true (T) or false (F), using the logic that if something is not necessarily true, then it is false.

    a. All white is good.
    b. Some black is yellow.
    c. Some red is bad.
    d. Some yellow is good.
    e. Some red is good.

5. Underline the odd one out in each of the following groups.

    a. abide, bear, stand, resist, remain
    b. promote, propose, advocate, foster, nourish
    c. swarthy, pale, blond, fair, light
    d. furtive, surreptitious, darkly, unauthorized, cheating
    e. mandatory, compulsive, overwhelming, uncontrollable, compelling
    f. confined, closed, bound, interned, incarcerated
    g. affect, bother, concern, effect, disturb
    h. condone, brook, commend, tolerate, excuse
    i. zenith, acme, vertex, nadir, climax
    j. hard, brittle, tough, leathery, rugged
    k. alight, embark, land, arrive, debark
    l. disdain, spurn, slight, deride, insult
    m. jilt, refuse, desert, drop, discard
    n. fear, shudder, quail, quiver, recoil
    o. beguile, entrap, enthral, thrill, engross

6. What number goes in the middle?

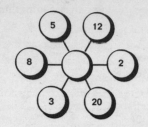

7. Identify the odd one out in each of the following.

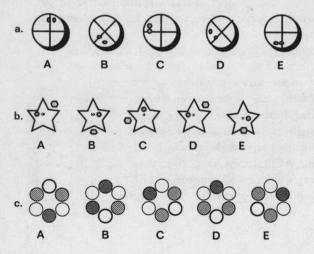

8. Underline the two words in each set that are closest to each other in meaning. Example: stand, <u>run</u>, hop, <u>jog</u>, dash.

    a. hit, stun, kill, shoot, thump
    b. nearly, hardly, exactly, precise, accurate
    c. vulnerable, safe, reliable, immune, secure
    d. grass, fauna, flora, nature, plants
    e. judgement, penalty, execution, conclusion, death
    f. requisition, collect, want, need, desire
    g. done, success, do, act, action
    h. forsake, faithful, remain, deny, portend
    i. shout, maintain, resume, complete, allege
    j. smelly, pungent, acrid, dull, aroma
    k. exactly, snobbery, prudence, vulnerability, care
    l. shame, alone, unhappy, bereft, desolate
    m. need, desperation, desire, destitution, must
    n. retain, derive, acquire, hunt, remain
    o. linguistic, conversant, ambiguous, multivocal, diverse

9. Insert the missing numbers.

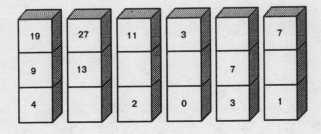

10. Which tile comes next?

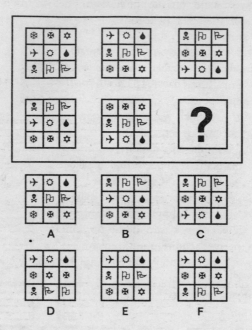

11. The bars on the following shapes represent numbers that, when added together, make the totals in the hexagons below. Insert the missing numbers in the blank hexagons.

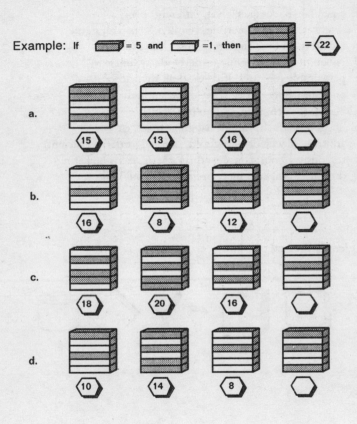

12. Identify the word within the brackets that is most nearly opposite in meaning to the first word. Example: pretty (clean, <u>ugly</u>, sharp, bad, naughty).

   a. equal (alike, coequal, rival, different, peer)
   b. erotic (rejecting, upsetting, swollen, venereal, sterile)
   c. regard (contempt, ignore, refuse, hurt, value)
   d. coherent (logical, senile, orderly, dotty, unclear)
   e. perceptible (obvious, hidden, dull, shy, closed)
   f. enchant (allure, repel, hate, deny, enthral)
   g. blanch (bleach, fade, boil, blush, faint)
   h. dogged (staunch, stupid, flagging, tenet, easy)
   i. arbitrary (decidedly, confused, rational, orderly, efficient)
   j. responsive (cool, concerned, apathetic, calm, uncaring)
   k. diabolical (wicked, nice, pretty easy, godlike)

13. Identify the odd one out.

A   B   C   D   E

14. In a chicken coop there are red, brown, white and yellow birds. Some of the brown birds are male, and some of the white birds are male, but none of the red birds is male. All of the yellow birds are female. All of the birds are fertile. State which of the following are true (T), false (F), and possible but not certain (P).

   a. All of the yellow birds can breed with some of the red birds.

   b. Some of the brown birds can breed with some of the red birds.

   c. Some of the white birds cannot breed with some of the white birds.

   d. All of the white birds can breed with some of the white birds.

   e. Some of the red birds can breed with some of the red birds.

   f. All of the yellow birds could breed with the fertile product of the mating of some of the brown birds.

   g. None of the yellow birds could breed with any of the white birds that could not breed with any of the red birds.

   h. There are more yellow birds of one sex than any of the other birds.

   i. Some of the brown birds cannot breed with some of the brown birds, or with any of the red birds or any of the yellow birds, but they can breed with some of the white birds and some of the brown birds.

   j. Some of the brown birds, some of the white birds, some of the yellow birds and some of the red birds cannot breed with some of the birds from any of these groups, but some of the colour groups have subgroups that can breed with birds from any of the groups.

15. Insert the missing numbers.

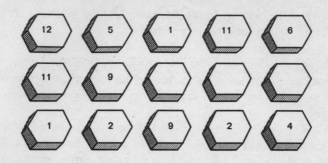

16. Complete the following sentence, selecting words from the list supplied. (Some of the words will not be needed.)

Necessity, it is said, is the mother of _____. When a desperate _____ arises, and _____ demand the _____ to a problem, the mind is _____ wonderfully, and we are _____ to action. It is during this time that we come up with our best _____, and instead of ignoring them, as we _____ do, we put them into _____.

situation, hope, always, mechanics, question, invention, cleared, solution, ideas, usually, forced, action, thinkers, working-order, concentrated, investigation, boxes, driven, people, must, inventing, many, children, circumstances, industry, people.

17. Complete the analogy.

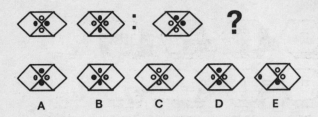

18. Insert the missing number.

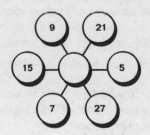

19. Which of the solutions below should replace the question mark? Balls can shift position within blocks but cannot move to blocks of a different colour.

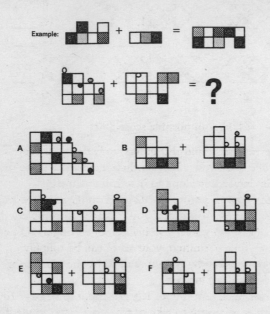

20. Find the prefixes that, when placed before each of the following groups of letters, will create valid words. Each set of words has a different prefix. Example: −ad, −acle, −ason, become tread, treacle and treason with the prefix tre−.

a. −ip, −avour, −ow, −ying, −oppy, −eet
b. −trary, −fusing, −cordant, −fidence, −science, −tract
c. −gale, −gard, −gain, −flect, −gime, −late
d. −port, −ply, −er, −pose, −plies, −per
e. −rdle, −rb, −ff, −rly, −b, −rse
f. −ny, −ost, −ld, −nd, −il, −ss
g. −k, −gry, −t, −ch, −ger, −dred
h. −t, −ve, −low, −e, −ted, −ient
i. −n, −re, −m, −rge, −aper, −p
j. −ll, −me, −na, −rp, −ld, −ef

Scoring – Check Your Gain

Mark your points here.

1. ___	6. ___	11. ___	16. ___
2. ___	7. ___	12. ___	17. ___
3. ___	8. ___	13. ___	18. ___
4. ___	9. ___	14. ___	19. ___
5. ___	10. ___	15. ___	20. ___

Total _____ (Maximum possible score 142)

To convert your total score into IQ points, read along the score line until you reach the mark you achieved, then draw a line up to meet the diagonal line and draw a line along to determine your IQ.

In the example shown, a score of 102 gives an IQ of about 130, + or − 5 points. As in the initial IQ test, if you managed to complete this test with great accuracy, scoring over 135 before converting to IQ points in much less than the time permitted, your score can be roughly extrapolated by multiplying by 60 and divided by the number of minutes taken to complete the test.

Again, as in the initial test, if your IQ works out to be over 130 on the scale above, you may wish to take a standardized test to see if you are eligible for membership in Mensa or other 'high IQ' organizations.

To determine your improvement using the first and final tests in this book use the formula: **New IQ score - original IQ score = Q**

Q ÷ 150 × 100 = percentage IQ improvement (+ or − approx 5%).

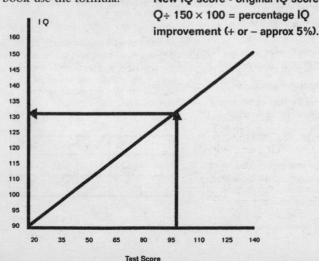

Answers

●●

IQ Test 1

1. (1 point each) a. mix; b. consider; c. more; d. throw; e. uppermost

2. (1 point each) a. Sunday; b. Thursday; c. Saturday; d. Saturday

3. (1 point each) a. 14 (1+4=5, 4+5=9, 5+9=14); b. 2 (47−1÷2=23, 23−1÷2=11, 11−1÷2=5, 5−1÷2=2); c. 44 (4x3=12, 4x5=20, 4x7=28, 4x9=36, 4x11=44); d. 21 (1+2=3, 3+4=7, 7+6=13, 13+8=21); e. 4 (79−39=40, 39−19=20, 19−9=10, 9−5=4); f. 11 (20−4=16, 16−5=11)

4. (1 point each) a. C (mirror image); b. B (the outside columns are reversed); c. B (the two grey squares are in a different position); d. C (the number of sides of each shape is indicated within it)

5. (1 point each correct word) Electricity is one of the cleanest and most **useful** sources of **energy** in our world, but it can be very **dangerous** to the unwary. It has a way of **seeking** out the careless or the indifferent and **punishing** them for their attitude.

6. (2 points) E

7. (1 point each) a. F; b. T; c. F; d. T; e. T; f. T; g. T; h. F; i. T; j. T; k. F

8. (1 point each) a. black; b. point; c. evening; d. hell; e. failure; f. certainty; g. property; h. southwest; i. optimistic; j. pluck; k. whisper; l. fail; m. abolish; n. body; o. evidence

9. (1 point each; all the answers are found by working in a clockwise direction from the top) a. 32; b. 62 (x2,+2); c. 81; d. 52 (5+8+13+26); e. 3 (÷2,+1); f. 5.5 (+1,÷2)

10. (1 point each prefix) a. glo– (gloat, global, gloom, glorify, glorious, glossy); b. be– (benign, besiege, best, belittle, bestow, bent); c. pu– (pure, purge, punch, punish, purity, puny); d. sk– (skill, skim, skinny, skirt, skulk, sky);

e. do– (doll, dope, dowry, dot, dock, door); f. spo–(spoof, spot, spotlit, spout, spoil, spook); g. bri– (bring, brink, bright, brisk, brittle, bribe); h. va– (vast, vault, vat, vary, vaunt, varied); i. bl– (blunt, blob, blue, blur, blink, blood); j. pa– (pact, pail, pan, paint, past, pale)

11. (1 point each) a. C (the arrow points in the way indicated by the letter R); b. D (the numbers in the other shapes indicate the total number of sides −1); c. C (the sizes of the cylinders are in proportion to the numbers); d. A (the label should be descriptive rather than instructional)

12. (1 point each) a. T; b. F (only five-twelfths of those that can fly are between one and two years old); c. P; d. T, e. F (there are three); f. F (there are four times as many); g. P; h. P; i. T; j. P; k. P; l. P

13. (1 point each) a. time; b. pain; c. talk; d. hold; e. tough; f. taste; g. altitude; h. foot; i. strike; j. emotion; k. aim; l. require; m. shift; n. strange; o. life

14. (1 point each) a. 500; b. 3,000; c. 3; d. 900; e. 500; f. 1,052; g. no

15. (3 points) B

16. (1 point each) The numbers in the top row are doubled to give the numbers in the middle row. The digits of the figures in the middle row are added together to give the numbers in the bottom row.

7	7.5	8.5	10.5	14.5
14	15	17	21	29
5	6	8	3	11

17. (1 point each)

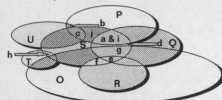

18. (1 point each) a. compare; b. invade; c. inseparably; d. stolid; e. drastic; f. devious; g. clarity; h. sort; i. fresh; j. satisfy; k. open; l. harmless

19. (1 point each) a. 1; b. 7 (+3,−4,+3,−4); c. 28 (4+3+7+14); d. 48 (2x4=8, 8x3=24, 24x2=48, 48x1=48); e. 65 (x2,−1,x2,−1); f. 0 (−4,−5,−6,−7); g. 4 (+1,÷2); h. 5 (÷2); i. 1 (square root); j. 8 (−10,−8,−6,−4); k. 284 (x3,−1); l. 142 (x2,+2)

20. (1 point each) a. B; b. C; c. A; d. D

VERBAL AND LINGUISTIC ABILITY – PRACTICE TEST 1

1. (1 point each) a. ostracize or ostracise; b. genesis (correct); c. fearful; d. excitement; e. exceedingly; f. sustenance; g. silhouette; h. diversion; i. soulless (correct); j. reminiscence (correct); k. effluent (correct); l. happening; m. formidable; n. pretentious (correct); o. regrettable (correct)

2. (1 point each word)

p	e	a	c	h
a	l	a	m	o
d	i	v	e	r
d	a	n	e	s
l	e	a	s	e
e	t	h	o	s

3. (1 point each; you can score for other solutions provided they are valid words) army, armed, armpit, armhole, armature, armadillo, Armageddon

4. (1 point each) a. Benjamin Franklin; b. Henry Wadsworth Longfellow; c. John Wesley; d. Oliver Goldsmith; e. Samuel Johnson; f. Julius Caesar

5. (1 point each) a. hand; b. eyes; c. feet; d. pencil; e. spade; f. book; g. door; h. rifle

6. (1 point each) a. curse; b. decide; c. precipitate; d. slender; e. convict

7. (1 point each word)

p	r	i	n	t
t	a	n	k	s
w	a	t	e	r
a	d	e	p	t
f	u	l	l	y
c	u	l	t	s
s	w	e	l	l
c	y	c	l	e
f	a	t	e	d

8. (1 point each) The following were correct: a, d, e, g, j, l, n, o, p, t, w, z. Look up the other words to make sure you know what they mean.

9. (1 point each) special, ordinary; b. desolate, cheerful; c. genuine, artificial; d. compel, deter; e. immaculate, contaminated; f. flabby, firm; g. bumpy, flat; h. appreciate, depreciate; i. seize, release; j. dirty, clean; k. understandable, perplexing

10. (1 point each) a. immediately; b. suppertime, c. find; d. trap; e. cowardly; f. sterile; g. indefinitely; h. seize; i. trick; j. hold; k. content; l. forgery

11. (1 point each) a. True *happiness* is of a retired *nature*, and an enemy to pomp and noise. It *arises*, in the first place, from the *enjoyment* of one's self, and, in the *next*, from the *friendship* and conversation of a *few* select *companions*. b. Sublime is the *dominion* of the mind over the *body*, that for a time, can make *flesh* and nerve *impregnable*, and string the sinews like *steel*, so that the *weak* become so mighty.

12. (1 point each word) The vertical word is confusion.

e	x	c	e	l
b	r	o	k	e
d	e	n	s	e
r	i	f	l	e
b	l	u	n	t
p	e	s	t	s
s	p	i	n	s
c	h	o	k	e
l	a	n	d	s

13. (1 point each word) a. Determine *exactly* what you are *going* to do in *return* for the *things* you *desire*. You *don't* get *anything* for *nothing* in *this* life. b. The *ultimate* goal in *life* must be the *acquisition* of *personal happiness* and *peace* of mind. *Go* for *it*! c. Among the most *successful* people in *industry*, the one *quality* that *most* of them *have* in common is *persistence*. Without that, *little* is *possible*. With it, *anything* is possible. d. Within every *unhappy* person is a *happy* person *waiting* to get out. Look deep *within* your *inner* being for the *happiness* and *joy* of life you were *born* with. It's *still* there *waiting* for *you*. e. If you *haven't* yet *established your* goals *in* life, then *you* are *unlikely* to *achieve* any of *them*. You *can't* plan for *what* you *don't* yet know you *want*.

14. (1 point each) a. frenzied; b. swollen; c. brag; d. preserve; e. beginning; f. cover; g. favour; h. fluid; i. reasoned; j. callous

15. (1 point each) a. big– (bigot, bigamist, bight, bigwig, bigger, bighorn); b. butter– (butterbean, butterfly, buttercup, buttermilk, butternut, butterfat); c. neu– (neural, neuritis, neuron, neuter, neutron, neutral); d. short– (shortage, shorts, shorter, shortening, shortly, shorten); e. vio– (violin, violet, violence, viola, violation, violent)

16. (1 point each word)

r	i	c	t	u	s
f	l	o	r	i	d
f	i	n	a	l	e
p	a	s	t	e	l
s	t	i	g	m	a
m	o	d	e	s	t
c	r	e	a	t	e
f	o	r	g	e	t
o	p	a	q	u	e
r	a	t	t	l	e
t	r	i	p	o	d
p	r	o	p	e	l
s	i	n	f	u	l

17. (1 point for 5 or more words in each group; 10 examples for each word are given, but there are many other possible rhymes) a. hair: chair, heir, lair, prayer, rare, snare, spare, stare, swear, their; b. flake: ache, break, fake, lake, quake, shake, snake, stake, take, wake; c. waiter: baiter, crater, debater, gaiter, greater, hater, later, pater, skater, slater; d. tail: fail, flail, gale, hail, mail, rail, sale, scale, snail, whale; e. drive: alive, arrive, chive, connive, derive, dive, five, hive, skive, strive; f. stumble: bumble, crumble, fumble, grumble, humble, jumble, mumble, rumble, scumble, tumble; g. aired: bared, blared, cared, fared, flared, glared, paired, scared, shared, snared

18. (1 point each) a. she; b. gut; c. enduring; d. invertebrate; e. zoom

19. (1 point each) dog – canine; wolf – lupine; fox – vulpine; cow – bovine; bear – ursine; fish – piscine

20. (5 points) All knowledge is itself of some value. There is nothing so minute or inconsiderable, that I would not rather know it than not. (Simply shift one place to the right on the keyboard so that, for example, t becomes y, p becomes a and m becomes q.)

21. (1 point each) a. ... and he'll take a yard (mile); b. ... for idle hands; c. ... is a friend to nobody; d. wisdom; e. ... to suck eggs; f. ... the heart doesn't grieve over; g. ... you need to be a friend; h. ... never won fair lady; i. ... than a dead hero; j. ... there's brass; k. ... and absolute power corrupts absolutely; l. ... the soul of wit; m. ... make good neighbours; n. ... 'twixt cup and lip; o. ... like success; p. ... in love and war; q. ... like an old fool; r. ... those who can't, teach; s. ... do it yourself; t. ... for a byway; u. ... quitters never win; v. ... bears little fruit; w. ... than an anvil; x. ... are those that never come; y. ... to a blind man (horse); z. ... repent at leisure

22. (1 point each word) To have a friend who is always *faithful*, never *angry*, always pleased to see you, never *deceitful*, ever loving, and who would give his or her life to *protect* you, you must either find your *soul-mate*, or buy a dog.

23. (1 point each word) The vertical word is wonderful.

p	o	w	e	r
p	h	o	n	e
b	o	n	n	y
d	a	d	d	y
p	r	e	s	s
e	a	r	t	h
i	n	f	e	r
f	a	u	l	t
s	i	l	l	y

24. (1 point each) a. calligraphy; b. computer; c. penalize or penalise; d. emollient; e. correspondence; f. achievement; g. perceive; h. manageable; i. tactful; j. harbinger; k. rancorous; l. vigorous; m. ingeniousness or ingenuousness; n. illiterately; o. mnemonically; p. rubaiyat or rubáiyát; q. practicable; r. fiascos; s. carcinogenic; t. beachcombers; u. phlegmatic; v. extravaganza; w. covetousness; x. lieutenant; y. locomotive; z. countenance

NUMERICAL PRACTICE TEST 1

1. a. 1 (+6); b. 18 (−1,×2); c. 38 (×2,+2); d. 165 (−2,×3); e. 152 (+10,+20,+40,+80); f. 27 (−6,×2,+1)

2. a. 45 minutes; b. 1 hour; c. 8 kilometres (40×12/60); d. 4 hours

3. 7

4. a. 9; b. 5; c. 32; d. 5; e. 11; f. 9 (The numbers at the top of each column indicate the positions of the digits in that column to give the result 1×2=3.)

5. 18 (Give the letters their numerical value according to alphabetical order.)

6. a. 19 (−10,+7); b. 12 (−3,+6); c. 18 (×2,−1); d. 31 (×3,−8); e. 160 (×5,−15)

7. C (Begin at top left and work anticlockwise. Let the first number be n and y be the difference between the first two numbers in the sequence. In the first set of numbers (1/3/5/9) y=2, so the sequence is n=1, n+y=3, n+2y=5, n+4y=9. Only C of the choices below follows this pattern.)

8. 4, 2, 21 (Give the letters their numerical value according to alphabetical order +1.)

9. a. 9 (38÷9=4, 2 over, 48÷9=5, 3 over); b. 6 (+4=10, 10×10=100, (100+4)÷4=26); c. 99 (÷3=33, ÷3=11, +11=22, −1=21, ÷7=3); d. 25 (÷5=5, ×3=15, +15=30, ÷10=3, ×3,×9=81)

10. 20

NUMERICAL PRACTICE TEST 2

1. 9

2. a. 1,290 kilometres; b. 1 hour, 34 minutes and 24 seconds (distance ÷ speed = 1290 ÷ (860−50) = 1.59 hours); c. 3 hours

3. a. 135 minutes (he uses 2 litres a minute); b. 180 minutes (he uses 1.5 litres a minute); c. 675 minutes (he uses 1 litre every 2½ minutes); d. 54 minutes (he uses 5 litres a minute)

4. The sequences are simple progressions: 7 in a, 5 in b and 8 in c.

a.

a10	c24	e38	g52	i66	k80
b17	d31	f45	h59	j73	l87

b.

a10	c20	e30	g40	i50	k60
b15	d25	f35	h45	j55	l65

c.

a9	c25	e41	g57	i73	k89
b17	d33	f49	h65	j81	l97

5.

1	4	9	5	2
9	5	2	1	4
2	1	4	9	5
4	9	5	2	1
5	2	1	4	9

6. 1 apple costs 10 credits; 1 banana costs 22 credits

$2a + 3b = 86$ and
$3a + 2b = 74$, therefore, by multiplying
$6a + 9b = 258$ and
$6a + 4b = 148$, therefore
$5b = 110$, therefore
$b = 22$, and, substituting
$a = 10$

7. Using the letters above each column as a key, a. (e×f)×2=gh; b. e×f−10=gh; c. ef+8=gh; d. (3×e)×h=fg; e. e×h=gf

a.

e	f	g	h
8	4	6	4
6	7	8	4
5	8	8	0
9	0	0	0

b.

e	f	g	h
3	5	0	5
9	4	2	6
8	6	3	8
2	9	0	8

c.

e	f	g	h
1	5	2	3
8	4	9	2
6	6	7	4
5	1	5	9

d.

e	f	g	h
3	6	3	7
8	4	8	2
6	5	4	3
5	7	5	5

e.

e	f	g	h
5	0	4	8
8	4	6	8
2	4	1	7
9	8	1	2

8. 2–13–26–20 (Map the alphabet against 1–26, starting, as indicated in the clue at f – f=1, g=2, etc. – and after z, begin with a=22, b=23, etc.)

9. a. 20–12–12–23 (Map the reversed alphabet, a=26, b=25, etc.); b. 5–17–16 (Using the letters c–o–n, map the alphabet beginning a=3, b=4, etc.); c. 13–4–11 (Using the letters n–e–l, map the alphabet beginning a=0, b=1, etc.)

10. David made the most frequent mistake in simple addition. For the radio-cassette he took 12.34 credits instead of 21.34 credits and for the wheel he took 16.91 credits instead of 19.61 credits. This is a difficult problem, which can be solved only by trial and error – so don't worry if you didn't get it.

NUMERICAL PRACTICE TEST 3

1.

3	4	1	8	9
1	8	9	3	4
9	3	4	1	8
4	1	8	9	3
8	9	3	4	1

2. a. 36 (18×2); b. 3 (9÷3); c. 64 (8×8); d. 7 (49÷7); e. 88 (44×2); f. 216 (12×18)

3. A simple repeating pattern.

6	6	5	5	4	4
7	7	8	8	9	9
12	12	11	11	10	10

4. a. 10 days; b. 15 days; c. on day 10; d. another 5 days

5. a. 10 sq m; b. 10 sq m

6. There are many possible ways of expressing these numbers, and only one example is given for each.
a. 23=3×4×2−1; b. 36=(1+3)×3×3; c. 11=(1×2×4)+3; d. 0=4−3+1−2; e. 3=1+(2×3)−4; f. 9=2×3−1+4

7. 4 July 1776 (The date of the American Declaration of Independence)

8. a. 3 minutes 20 seconds; b. 1 minute 40 seconds; c. 27.5 litres

9. 100 (For every five steps he takes, he progresses one; 5×20=100.)

10. a. 192 sq m; b. 12m; c. 76m (include the section about B); d. 480

VISUAL–SPATIAL PRACTICE TEST 1

1. C, F

2. D (the solid black and grey shapes have switched)

3. C

4. a. D (a hammer is not necessarily a weapon); b. D (the numbers written on the other shapes are the number of faces ×2); c. C (the figure beneath should be 8, given that light boxes are worth 1 and dark boxes 2); d. A (there are 4 shapes)

5. 11

6. E (each shape turns anticlockwise through 90 degrees)

7. E

8. D

9. a. C; b. A

10. i is wrong and should be replaced by A

VISUAL–SPATIAL PRACTICE TEST 2

1.

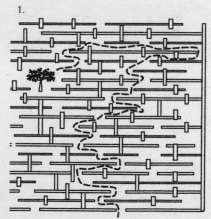

2. A

3. Thinkers – telephone, hammer, I (eye), notes, key, elephant, rabbit, scissors

4. a. B; b. apart; c. together; d. apart; e. apart

5. a. D; b. C (not symmetrical); c. C (software not hardware)

6. C

7. D

8. B (The top rows of the tiles follow the sequence, 123, 234, 345 and so on, with the numbering running from left to right, right to left and left to right.)

9. D (The others are hexagons.)

10. C (Compare the balls and count the coloured squares.)

LOGICAL DEDUCTION PRACTICE TEST 1

(Score 1 point for each part of an answer unless otherwise indicated.)

1. 70

2. Mary

3. (1 point) red 1; yellow 2; blue 3; pink 4; green 5

4. Fish

5. a. T; b. F (there is no way of determining the children's weight); c. F (there would have to be 24 girls for this to be true); d. F (their mental state cannot be assessed); e. T; f. T

6. F (The Venn diagram shows that the tables that can eat could be isolated within the group of dreams. Unless you know that the tables that can eat intrude into the group of pianos that can walk, you cannot assume that it is so.)

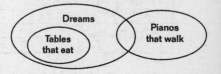

7. a. F (the speed at which an object drops depends on the pull of gravity not on its weight nor, in the absence of atmos-

phere, on size or shape); b. F (whatever its weight, the black ball will not defy gravity); c. F (both balls will fall); d. T (the balls could have been treated in some way that makes them explode and so, according to the laws of Martian logic, the statement is not necessarily false and must be regarded as true); e. T (objects fall at the same speed in the absence of atmospheric interference); f. T (a thrown ball will travel further in lower gravity)

8. a. Ricardo; b. Suzanne; c. Jon

9. a. day 6; b. day 5; c. day 4

10. She needs to know what the watches are worth unrepaired; she needs to know if she could sell them more easily as a pair or singly. If the total value of the unrepaired watches is more that 120 credits, she would do better to sell them as they are. If their total unrepaired value is less than 120 credits, her decision will depend on how easily she will be able to sell the watches.

LOGICAL DEDUCTION PRACTICE TEST 2

(Score 1 point for each part of an answer unless otherwise indicated.)

1. (5 points) This is a matter of trial and error.

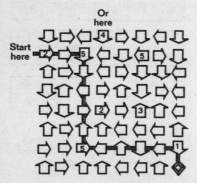

2. (10 points) Many people take no care of their money until they have come nearly to the end of it, and others do just the same with their time. Their best days they throw away, let them run like sand through their fingers, as long as they think they have an almost countless number of them to spend; but when they find their days flowing rapidly away, so that at last they will have very few left, then they will at once make a very wise use of them; but unluckily they have by that time no notion how to do it.

3. a. F; b. F; c. T; d. F (we do not know how many pairs she has altogether); e. T; f. F; g. T; h. T

4. a. F; b. F; c. F; d. F; e. T; f. T; g. T; h. F; i. F

5. a. Sandy, Michael, Andrew; b. Sheila is 12, Fred is 3, Anne is 1, Lorraine is 10, Sean is 4

6. a. 39 days; b. 38 days

7. (5 points) 1, 2, 4 and 8 (1, 2, 1+2, 4, 4+1, 4+2, 4+1+2, 8, 8+1, 8+2, 8+1+2, 8+4, 8+4+1, 8+4+2, 8+4+1+2)

8. (5 points) It is not enough simply to say that arrows do not understand the paradox and would travel to their targets regardless. The following explanation (or one based on the same lines) is the only valid refutation of the paradox that has been found. Let the distance travelled be 1, in the given time 1. No matter how small the division of that distance, 1, the arrow has an equally small division of the time unit 1 in which to travel that distance, and all the divisions of time and of distance total 1, rather than infinity.

9. a. Mark, Jack, Kevin, Lana; b. Mark, Lana, Kevin, Jack; c. Jack, Lana, Kevin, Mark

10. (4 points) Suspend the board from one point and draw a vertical line from the support point. Suspend it from another point and draw another vertical line. Where the lines intersect is the centre of balance.

LOGICAL DEDUCTION PRACTICE TEST 3

(Score 1 point for each part of an answer unless otherwise indicated.)

1. (5 points each) a. tmbwf (Map 'slave' one place to the right in the alphabet.) b. 1221288 (Map the alphabet in reverse numerical order – a=26, b=25 and so on – and when double numbers occur, delete the second digit – i.e., j=17=1.)

2. (4 points) 5 cards (47 is the only number that gives the correct remainders each time.)

3. (4 points) Diamond = 4; hexagon = 3; oval = 7; triangle = 6

4. (10 points for finding all the words; deduct 1 point for each word not found) 1. den; 2. crash; 3. hurt; 4. rush; 5. hi; 6. inside; 7. train; 8. hit; 9. spot; 10. outside; 11. trips; 12. pig; 13. easily; 14. elastic; 15. arsenic; 16. alone; 17. lost; 18. tennis; 19. totally; 20. daring; 21. decider; 22. idle; 23. run; 24. Isis; 25. lay; 26. she; 27. racer; 28. line; 29. rose; 30. shoes; 31. hoe; 32. opium; 33. print; 34. crow; 35. trees; 36. sir; 37. spin; 38. rap; 39. pie; 40. Eros; 41. ion; 42. rug; 43. hip; 44. sin; 45. carrot; 46. bun; 47. step; 48. sons; 49. lament; 50. chairs; 51. psychology; 52. ecology; 53. York; 54. coons; 55. show

5. (1 point each) Jake 60; his son 33; his grandson 9; his granddaughter 13; Newton 8; Galileo 6

6. No

7. amplify, enlarge, expand, develop; expansion, growth, increment, swelling; diminish, contract, shrink, reduce; reduction, shrivelling, elision, constriction

8. a. F; b. F; c. T; d. P; e. F; f. F; g. F; h. T; i. F; j. P

9. 66.66 metres (4/60 of a kilometre)

10. a. 330 (390−(4×15)); b. 378 (330+(4×12)); c. 315 (330−75+60)

GENERAL KNOWLEDGE

Set 1: 1. b; 2. c; 3. a; 4. a; 5. b; 6. a; 7. a; 8. a; 9. b; 10. c

Set 2: 1. b; 2. b; 3. c; 4. a; 5. a; 6. c; 7. c; 8. b; 9. c; 10. a

Set 3: 1. a; 2. b; 3. a; 4. a; 5. c; 6. a; 7. c; 8. a; 9. a; 10. b

Set 4: 1. a; 2. c; 3. b; 4. b; 5. b; 6. b; 7. a; 8. c; 9. a; 10. b

Set 5: 1. b; 2. b; 3. c; 4. c; 5. c; 6. a; 7. c; 8. b; 9. c; 10. b

Set 6: 1. b; 2. a; 3. c; 4. b; 5. a; 6. a; 7. b; 8. a; 9. a; 10. c

Set 7: 1. c; 2. b; 3. b; 4. a; 5. b; 6. c; 7. a; 8. a; 9. b; 10. b

Set 8: 1. a; 2. a; 3. b; 4. b; 5. c; 6. b; 7. c; 8. c; 9. c; 10. b

Set 9: 1. a; 2. c; 3. c; 4. b; 5. b; 6. a; 7. b; 8. c; 9. b; 10. a

Set 10: 1. a; 2. a; 3. b; 4. a; 5. a; 6. c; 7. b; 8. a; 9. b; 10. c

IQ Test 2

1. (1 point each) a. luggage; b. reptile; c. book; d. weapon; e. tool; f. person; g. vehicle; h. pig; i. ship; j. appendage; k. hat; l. footwear; m. colour; n. quantity; o. category

2. The sequences are simple progressions: (a) a×b=c, d×e=f and so on; (b) a+b=c, c+d=e and so on; (c) a−b=c, d−e=f and so on.

a.

a2	c4	e3	g4	i16	k5
b2	d3	f9	h4	j5	l25

b.

a1	c3	e8	g21	i55	k144
b2	d5	f13	h34	j89	l233

c.

a15	c14	e2	g13	i10	k4
b1	d14	f12	h3	j12	l8

3. (3 points) C, E

4. (1 point each) a. F; b. F; c. T; d. F; e. F

5. (1 point each) a. resist; b. propose; c. swarthy, d. darkly; e. mandatory; f. closed; g. effect; h. commend; i. nadir; j. brittle; k. embark; l. insult; m. refuse; n. fear; o. entrap

6. (1 point) 4

7. (1 point each) a. B; b. C; c. B

8. (1 point each pair) a. hit, thump;
b. precise, accurate; c. safe, secure;
d. flora, plants; e. judgement, conclusion; f. want, desire; g. do, act;
h. forsake, deny; i. maintain, allege;
j. pungent, acrid; k. prudence, care;
l. bereft, desolate; m. need, desire;
n. derive, acquire; o. ambiguous, multivocal

9. (1 point each) The bottom line × 2 + 1
= middle line × 2 + 1 = top line

19	27	11	3	15	7
9	13	5	1	7	3
4	6	2	0	3	1

10. (3 points) F

11. (1 point each) a. 14; b. 10; c. 14; d. 12

12. (1 point each) a. different; b. sterile;
c. contempt; d. unclear; e. hidden;
f. repel; g. blush; h. flagging;
i. rational; j. apathetic; k. godlike

13. (1 point) A (viewed from above)

14. (1 point each) a. F ; b. T; c. T; d. P; e.
F; f. P; g. T; h. P; i. T; j. T (One of the
best ways of testing these statements is
by means of a Venn diagram.)

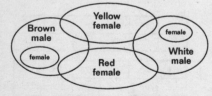

15. (1 point each) The numbers in the middle row are the product of the numbers
in top and bottom row −1.

12	5	1	11	6
11	9	8	21	23
1	2	9	2	4

16. (1 point each) Necessity, it is said, is the
mother of **invention**. When a desperate **situation** arises, and **circumstances** demand the **solution** to a
problem, the mind is **concentrated**
wonderfully, and we are **driven** to
action., It is during this time that we
come up with our best **ideas**, and
instead of ignoring them, as we **usually**
do, we put them into **action**.

17. (3 points) B

18. (1 point) 3

19. (3 points) C

20. (2 points each) a. fl− (flip, flavour, flow,
flying, floppy, fleet); b. con− (contrary,
confusing, concordant, confidence,
conscience, contract); c. re− (regale,
regard, regain, reflect, regime, relate); d.
sup− (support, supply, super, suppose,
supplies, supper); e. cu− (curdle, curb,
cuff, curly, cub, curse); f. bo− (bony,
boost, bold, bond, boil, boss); g. hun−
(hunk, hungry, hunt, hunch, hunger,
hundred); h. sal− (salt, salve, sallow, sale,
salted, salient); i. di− (din, dire, dim,
dirge, diaper, dip); j. chi− (chill, chime,
china, chirp, child, chief)

USEFUL ADDRESSES

For further information about Mensa,
contact:

UK/Ireland
British Mensa Ltd
Mensa House
St John's Square
Wolverhampton WV2 4AH

USA
American Mensa Ltd
2626 East 14th Street
Brooklyn
New York
NY 11235–3992

Australia
Australian Mensa Incorporated
PO Box 213
Toorak
Victoria

For information about Mensa in
countries not listed please contact:

Mensa International Ltd
15 The Ivories
6–8 Northampton Street
London N1 2HY